THE SUCCESSFUL ENTREPRENEUR PLAYBOOK

A PRACTICAL GUIDE TO BUILDING A SUCCESSFUL BUSINESS

PAUL H. WOODRUFF

Publishing Services provided by Paper Raven Books LLC

Printed in the United States of America

First Printing, 2022

Paperback ISBN: 979-8-9872005-0-6

Hardback ISBN: 979-8-9872005-1-3

DEDICATION

This book is dedicated to Marcia, my wife and the love of my life. Without her urging, this book wouldn't have been written.

ACKNOWLEDGEMENTS

It is difficult to identify and thank all those who contributed to this book. With that said, I want to thank Bill Yoh, an author and former executive at Day, and Zimmerman Inc., who helped me think through what this book was going to be about. To the beta readers: Berta Aldrich, author of *Winning the Talent Shift* and a senior executive in several major companies; Andrej Avalini, a Principal with AEC Advisors, LLC; Arnon Garonzik, an independent consultant and former General Counsel and Director of ERM's South American operations; Marcos Lopez, Founder and CEO of Exude, Inc.; Bob Purcell, Founder and President of Beachwood Custom Builders, Inc.; and Dan Sevick, former president of Roskamp Management, LLC and CFO of ERM—thank you for your time and numerous suggestions that improved this book. I want to say a special thank you to Randy Lindel for his significant contributions to Chapter 6. I'm especially grateful to Nikki Burrell, whose patience and skills were integral in producing this book as she transcribed hours of dictation and my semi-legible handwritten edits. Kudos to my daughter, Joy Ramirez, for her numerous assists when my digital technology skills failed me. Hats off also to my editors and publishers at Paper Raven Books for their support and guidance in bringing this book to fruition. Last, but not least, I want to thank my wife, Marcia, without whose urging this book wouldn't have happened, for her indulgence in the hours I spent writing it.

TABLE OF CONTENTS

Dedication iii

Acknowledgements v

Table of Contents vii

Prologue ix

CHAPTER 1 – Becoming an Entrepreneur 1

CHAPTER 2 – Getting Started 11

CHAPTER 3 – Dealing with Legal Organizational Forms and Taxes 21

CHAPTER 4 – Crafting a Business Plan 28

CHAPTER 5 – Finding and Keeping Employees 34

CHAPTER 6 – Marketing and Sales 61

CHAPTER 7 – Recognizing and Managing Major Business Risks 79

CHAPTER 8 – Delivering the Goods and Services 94

CHAPTER 9 – Creating and Managing Growth 101

CHAPTER 10 – Making a Profit 112

CHAPTER 11 — Growing Your Ability to Succeed 120

CHAPTER 12 — Growing Internationally 128

CHAPTER 13 — Exiting Your Business 131

CHAPTER 14 — Sharing Some Final Thoughts 141

Further Reading 143

APPENDIX 1 144

APPENDIX 2 148

APPENDIX 3 150

PROLOGUE

In the following, the author provides a brief overview of his journey as an entrepreneur in building a global environmental consulting business.

I always wanted a business of my own. In the fall of 1977, I set out to make it happen.

From the very beginning, I intended to develop a national environmental consulting company specializing, initially, in hazardous waste management. I recognized that with limited capital, I needed to find a nontraditional way to grow a business. One way to accomplish this was to establish regional businesses, each individually managed and partially owned by qualified professionals.

This form of organization worked very well for a friend, as he was developing life care communities across the United States. I also saw how other service-related businesses, such as national real estate chains and some law firms, seemed to be organized in the same or a similar fashion. Only many years later did I discover that J.C. Penney built his chain of over a thousand retail stores using the same model. I also learned Benjamin Franklin established print shops that were affiliated with his business along the eastern seaboard and into the Caribbean, but I did not know that at the time. This model allowed me to take advantage of my contacts that were national in scope, both among clients and prospective partners. At 40 years old, I recognized that this market would develop rapidly, and I knew I had to find a mechanism to allow us to grow quickly if we were to become one of the principal players in this field.

There were several lessons my previous employment taught me (both positive and negative) that I employed in developing our business and organizational model. Among them were the following:

- **People work best when they work for themselves.** They inherently have to take ownership for success or failure.

- **Each region of the country has its own flavor.** Success comes easier if the leadership is already in place in that region and they already developed a regional reputation, bringing client and staff contacts and an understanding of the way people think and work. This is also a cheaper model in that you are not relocating people and their families and bearing the cost of training people in a new area. Partners and employees with significant "skin in the game" are likely to be more diligent workers and better at balancing risk and reward than those who do not.

- **Staff turnover in our industry was a major problem.** Because the environmental field was new, universities were not turning out graduates fast enough to keep up with the demand for their skills. Finding and keeping experienced personnel was a major challenge for all employers. By providing a business model where key individuals have serious ownership opportunities and minimal need to relocate to foster their careers, together with a philosophy that values individuality, creativity, and participatory-type management, we could attract and keep the best people.

- **Each region is encouraged to become a fully developed business unit, while at the same time taking advantage of complementary skills and depth available in other regions.** This contrasted with my previous employer's model, where the most experienced people were located at "headquarters."

- **Each regional business unit should perform those tasks at the regional level that best and most efficiently could be accomplished there.** I wanted a structure with minimal overhead and a way to eliminate the cost and conflict that are inevitable when individual business units are required to pay for costs they have no control over.

- **I recognized the necessity of building a structure that I could not, in the face of overwhelming opposition by my partners, force my will upon.** This was probably one of the hardest facets for outsiders to appreciate, but I knew that my judgment was not infallible. I anticipated times when I needed to be saved from myself. This also enabled me to attract strong, able partners because they knew collectively they had real power.

STARTUP PHASE

I began to take the mechanical steps necessary to incorporate a company. I obtained a $10,000 (equivalent to about $50,000 in 2022 dollars) bank loan on my personal signature. It was the seed capital for Environmental Resources Management, Inc. (hereafter, I'll refer to the company as ERM or the ERM Group). I arbitrarily decided my reputation, contacts, and experience were worth $100,000 (or about $500,000 currently) as a basis for valuing ERM. With that figure in mind, I intended to bring in partners and sell them a piece of the business.

I felt the most promising current and future opportunity in the environmental consulting field was hazardous waste. Even before the United States Congress passed the Resources Recovery and Conservation Act (RCRA) in 1976, it became apparent to me this was a growing concern to industry and regulators. To be competitive in this market, I knew we needed a multi-disciplinary team, including civil and chemical engineers, hydrogeologists, geochemists, toxicologists, and related specialists. There were no established competitors. It was with this market in mind that I selected my original partners.

I looked for talented individuals who could help me sell work. I wanted people with the ability in the early years to perform the work and later who could recruit and manage others. I also needed to find professionals with complementary experience to mine. In October 1977, I welcomed my first partner and agreed to sell him 15 percent of the business for $15,000. We planned to reinvest that $15,000, which was retained by the company as part of our startup capital, along with the $10,000 I already invested.

In January 1978, I brought on my second partner and second 15 percent stakeholder. ERM commenced operations on January 1, 1978, although I incorporated the business in Pennsylvania on October 10, 1977—my 40th birthday. For a short time, we worked out of our homes. In the spring, we leased space in a newly constructed office building in a nearby town.

Our little company took off. We continued to find new clients and little by little added staff. My third senior partner arrived in September. Over the next couple of years, I recruited two more key men to round out our team of original partners. This was an exhilarating time for me. I somehow knew that we could succeed, but it was great to see it happening.

Before the year's end, our client list grew to include several Fortune 500 companies, as well as some smaller industry clients. I landed our first international project working for a U.S.-based Fortune 500 company developing a new manufacturing plant in Cork, Ireland, and shortly thereafter, we successfully won additional work in the States. With the business foundation in place, I started to concentrate on bringing in new clients and implementing my plan to grow our business.

GROWING NATIONALLY

Shortly after launching ERM, I contacted a former associate who managed a regional office in the Southwest. I wanted to see if he had any interest in joining me. His initial response was, "No," but on a subsequent call, his answer was positive. Thus began a dialogue and negotiations over specifics on him joining the team and establishing a new affiliate with half a dozen states as its territory.

When I first started ERM, I retained an attorney to prepare a shareholder agreement. I knew it was important to identify the rights and obligations of those who invested money in the firm. That shareholder agreement then became the basis for all of the subsequent companies we established. The business model that I worked out was as follows. My affiliate partner or partners owned 50 percent of the company and contributed their share of the startup capital in cash or by agreeing to work for an extended period at either no salary or a partial salary (until they contributed their 50 percent share). It was my partners' responsibility to find additional business partners, subject to my approval, with complementary talents and skills to help grow our business.

In addition, the two founding 50-percent owners agreed to sell stock to new regional shareholders until the founding owners diluted down to a 33-percent ownership interest. This agreement proved to be a significant driving force in growing the regional business by providing an equity driver for the next generation of key staff.

Another financial ingredient in the affiliate relationships provided each regional company with a basket of services from their corporate partner. Some of these services were free, such as the time ERM, Inc. employees devoted to helping the regional companies grow their businesses. Some services were charged on a direct reimbursement basis for outside costs, such as employee benefit plans, developing and printing sales literature, advertising, business insurance, etc. By handling these overhead costs required to run the business in this way, we avoided elaborate accounting and almost eliminated intercompany disagreements with respect to parent-partner overhead.

Over the next few years, we set up additional affiliate companies. In one case, a regional company started with an existing business when we acquired a 50-percent interest. The last domestic affiliate to complete the coverage of the U.S. market was set up in the Pacific Northwest. Each of our regional companies was typically incorporated in the state where its principal office was located. Each had a Board of Directors consisting of one or more of my regional partners and myself. As the number of companies grew, I encouraged other corporate partners to join me as directors. We typically met quarterly with meetings that often lasted most of the day.

The original company that I established, ERM, Inc., was, for the first ten years or so, both a holding company with equity in each of its affiliates and also a regional operating company.

All of our companies were set up as "C-Personal Service Corporations" and cash-basis taxpayers. It proved to be very advantageous as it allowed us to defer paying taxes, which left us with more working capital. Unfortunately, the U.S. Congress passed new legislation in 1986 that required the parent company to become an accrual taxpayer. With the help of our outside advisors, we created an alternative organization that allowed all of the companies to remain cash-basis taxpayers. We converted all of the companies to "S" corporations, which we qualified for, to continue to utilize the cash basis for tax purposes.

After we separated the holding company from the regional operating business, each of these entities comprised a Board of Directors and Officers. I continued serving as Chairman of the Board for ERM-Mid Atlantic, the new regional operating company; Chairman, President, and CEO of The ERM Group, the parent investment entity; and Chairman of the Board of each of the other regional companies.

RAPID GROWTH

After a short period of building a critical mass, growth exploded. We calculated that between 1977 and 1990, the business grew at a compound rate of 80-plus percent per year. Even in the rapidly burgeoning area of environmental consulting, this was an unheard-of growth rate. I believe this exceptional growth rate was due to several factors. First, we were able to attract exceptionally talented people and experienced almost no turnover at the partner level and much less than our competitors at the staff level. Second, our businesses were extremely profitable, which provided the capital to grow, as well as to provide extraordinary cash incentives for the partners and bonuses for staff. Third, we used a three-dimensional growth model, with growth through geographical expansion, expanding services, and expanding our client base. Our regional structure allowed us to grow on many fronts geographically at the same time. Most of our regions established branch offices in key markets within their regions. We continued to expand the new services' niches. Once we established a track record in one niche, then we purposely transplanted the capability into as many regions and offices as possible. This allowed us to perform a wider spectrum of work for our existing client base, as well as helped us bring in new clients. Finally, we focused mostly on Fortune 1000 clients, most of whom had multiple divisions operating from many locations. We worked hard to penetrate across business lines with each of our clients.

One of the measures of our growth was a survey each year by *Inc. Magazine* that published a list of the 500 fastest-growing companies in the United States. We made that list five out of six years (1984–1989), which at the time had only been accomplished by one other firm. We were recognized for our rapid growth by several other organizations, including the Philadelphia Business Council, as the Firm of the Year in 1994. I was recognized as Entrepreneur of the Year in 1989 by the same organization.

Some of the new services we added were encapsulated in separate companies. This included environmental remediation construction businesses (these operated as regional companies in parallel with their consulting company partners) intended to isolate the greater risk associated with construction. We set up a couple of analytical laboratories, a catastrophic risk assessment company, an occupational health and safety practice, one other that focused on environmental toxicology, and two that provided other companies with temporary environmental staffing. We also developed drilling businesses to determine groundwater and soil contaminants, as well as a company with a digitized database of federal and state environmental regulations on a subscription basis. We also established a construction dispute resolution firm, a financial advisory, merger and acquisition company specializing in the environmental area, and a captive insurance company to provide professional liability coverage for our businesses.

ERM EXPANDS INTERNATIONALLY

Our first international company was established in Canada. Not long after that, one of my partners introduced me to Environmental Resources, LTD (ERL), a United Kingdom (UK)-based environmental consulting firm. The firm's founder, Florence Fisher, decided to find a "white knight" to buy her company away from a large UK-based conglomerate that recently had acquired an engineering firm that, only a short time before, she had sold out to. We crafted the deal such that ERM, Inc. owned 85 percent of the company. The local partners were given 15 percent and the opportunity to be given an additional 15 percent if certain goals were met. This turned out to be one of the best acquisitions we made.

By 1986, we established regional companies in 11 markets that filled out the U.S. continental 48 states, as shown in Figure 1. I initially set a goal to establish 10 regional businesses in 10 years. It only took nine years, and as noted, we created 11.

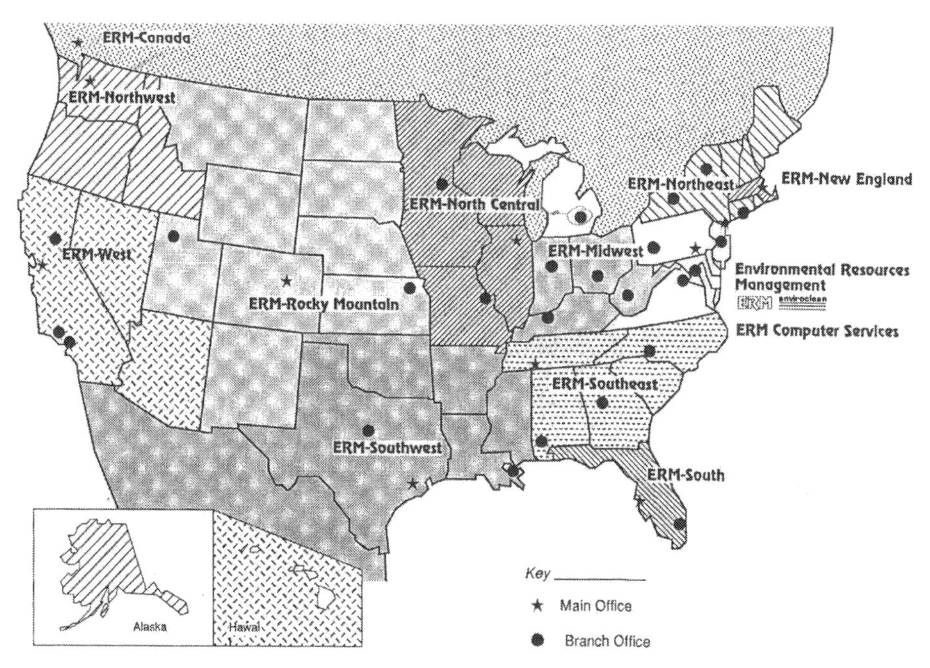

Figure 1: The Environmental Resources Management Group of Companies

The timing was perfect. I had the time and energy now to develop the international side of our business. Part of the rationale for moving internationally was to defend our position in our domestic marketplace. About the time of my initial meeting with the principals of ERL, three clients asked us to assist them with environmental problems at overseas locations. In each case, we prepared proposals but lost out to competitors because they had staff somewhat proximate to the project, and we couldn't compete due to the extra burden of travel and the higher cost of American salaries. This felt like a message to which we needed to respond. Many, if not most, of our Fortune 1000 clients had affiliates, subsidiaries, or operating plants in geographic markets outside the United States.

We formulated a plan to identify partners in the major European countries. We started in Germany by transferring one of my original partners, Peter Klose, who was born in what was to become Eastern Germany and immigrated to the United States as a young boy. He spoke fluent German. He asked for the opportunity. We eventually located additional partners and set up affiliates in Belgium, Italy, France, Portugal, Scotland, the Netherlands, Spain, Hungary, and Poland.

Asia and the Pacific Rim became our next targets. ERL had an office in Hong Kong. We made a significant acquisition in Australia to establish a base of operations in this country. The company in Taiwan resulted from combining the talents of an American in Taipei, whom I knew from my previous job, and a mainland Chinese man, who obtained his Ph.D. in the United States and also lived in Taipei. Eventually, companies were established in China, Singapore, Malaysia, Thailand, Japan, India, Indonesia, and Korea. In each case (except China), we started with one or two individuals, usually from that country.

In some cases, our initial inoculation in a country didn't work out; in other words, our initial choice of key managers didn't produce the results we had hoped for. One such case was in India. An Indian entrepreneur who lived in the Madras area, now called Chennai, contacted me about setting up an ERM affiliate in India. After protracted conversations, including face-to-face meetings both here and in India, we decided to proceed. However, in time, it became apparent that what he had in mind was to develop a small, family-controlled entity into which he could bring one or both of his sons. This is a very traditional Indian approach to business. Ultimately, we decided to part company and start again with a base in New Delhi.

We initiated our business interest in South America with the company we set up in Brazil. In this case, I looked at several companies that I thought might be potential partners before settling on a small Brazilian manufacturing company that had started an environmental consulting business. The owner of the manufacturing business was a relatively young man when his father died, and he took over. He was a graduate of The Harvard Business School and had some very unorthodox management ideas, particularly for Brazil. He had a flair for publicity, and due to his controversial, yet successful ideas, he became quite a high-profile individual in the Brazilian business community. He found a PhD-level environmental engineer to lead a small environmental consulting group. They were in São Paolo, and eventually, offices were established in Rio de Janeiro. ERM acquired half of this consulting firm and changed its name to ERM Brazil. Later, other companies in ERM's Latin American and Caribbean regions were established in Argentina, Chile, and Puerto Rico. Additionally, ERM-Southwest, headquartered in Texas, established a consulting business with multiple offices in Mexico.

Figures 2 and 3 show ERM's growth in revenue and employees, respectively, over the years. The ownership structure of the ERM Group of companies, which was known internally as a spider diagram, is shown in Figure 4. Figure 5 shows ERM Global locations from around 2000.

As the number of regional companies was growing, it became increasingly necessary to bring the senior partners in each of these companies together to ensure everyone knew one another and to take care of group business. I made the decision early on to include spouses for several reasons. I thought it was important that the spouses know the senior partners with whom their husbands or wives worked. I also felt it was a small reward, to include spouses and give them a company-paid mini-holiday, for the extra hours that these partners committed to our company. Meetings were usually held once a year and always in a special location. Initially, for the first ten years or so, we met somewhere in the United

States. Eventually, as we added more international partners, we switched to a location overseas and held the meeting every two or three years.

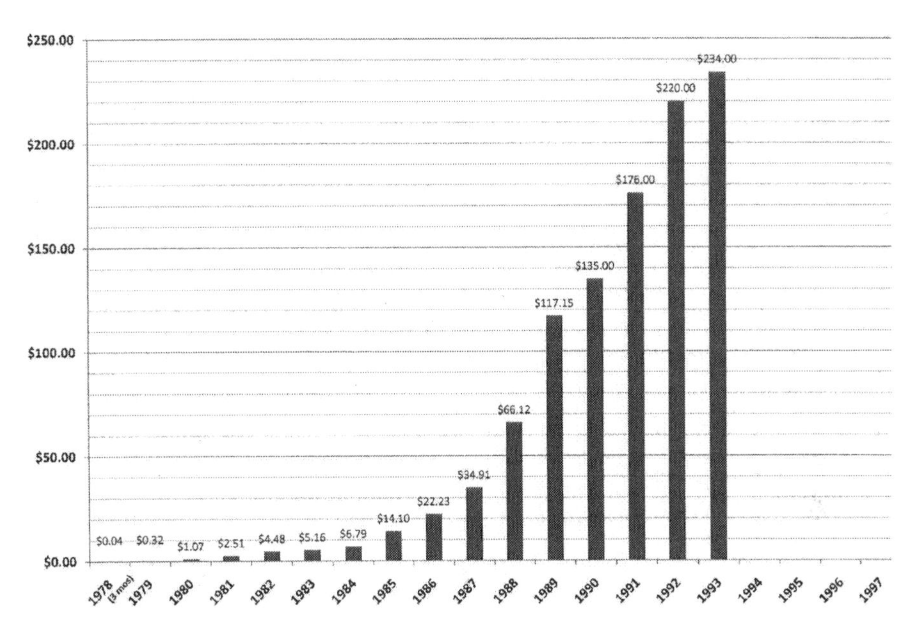

Figure 2: ERM's growth in revenue

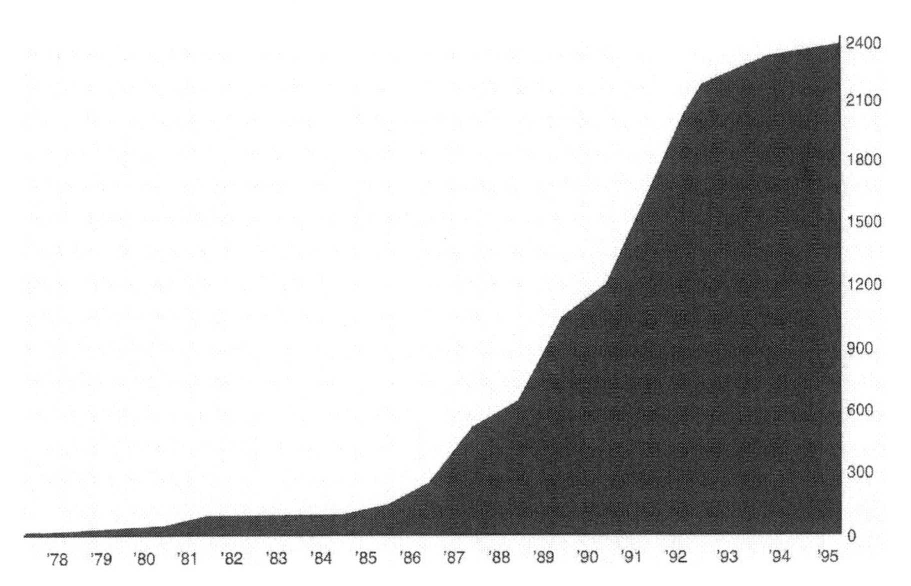

Figure 3: ERM's growth in employees (1977-1995)

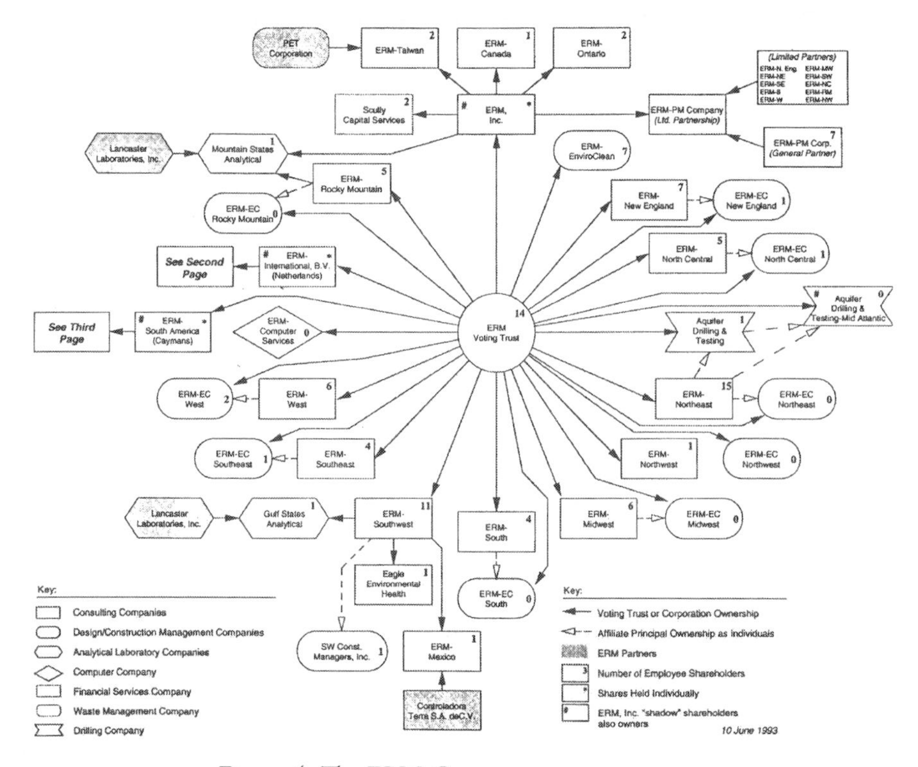

Figure 4: The ERM Group - corporate structure

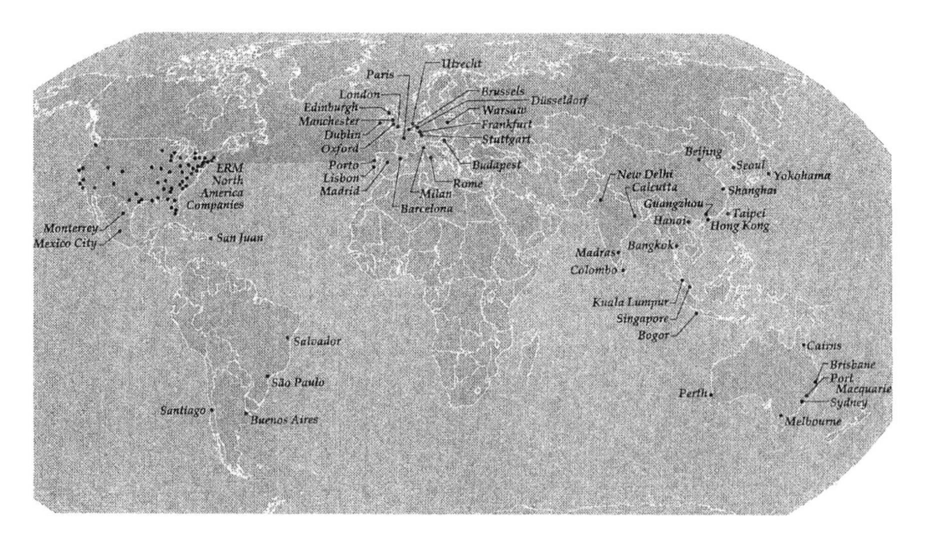

Figure 5: ERM locations in the world

We established holding companies for our businesses outside of the United States. A Cayman Island-based company held our interests in South America. We had a UK-based holding company that held our interests in Europe and the Asian-Pacific regions of the world. I changed the formula a bit concerning local ownership in setting up these offshore companies. As an example, the principal partners in the affiliate in France owned up to one-third of that business, with the remaining two-thirds held by the ERM-Europe holding company in the UK. The original plan was to encourage the local partners to then purchase an interest in their holding company, but this proved to be impractical. My U.S.-based original ERM, Inc. partners and I owned the majority of the offshore holding companies. In this way, the original partners controlled the international companies. Although it was a complex, decentralized structure, it served its purpose in that it maximized local partner incentives to succeed and retained talented partners. It made it very difficult, however, to explain to outsiders, including our banks, and to recapitalize or sell my interest. Our business grew to 66 companies with offices and staff in 34 countries and 121 locations by 2001.

In the mid-1990s, I formed an advisory board for the ERM Group of companies that met quarterly. I recruited some outstanding people, and I also encouraged insiders to regularly participate. They all were extremely helpful to me. They forced me to think about the major issues facing our businesses in preparation for our meetings. After five years, I disbanded the board, as several members were having difficulty attending.

MY EXIT FROM ERM

I ultimately began to think about succession and transitioning ownership. As time went on, it became increasingly apparent that we needed to find a way to encourage greater standardization and collaboration between individual companies. As an example, most of our companies decided on the type of software they used for their accounting systems and new business initiatives. It was very difficult for management in each company to collectively focus their energies on specific services or market initiatives. These drawbacks had not been serious enough to impact our growth because of the offsetting advantages to our structure, but I could see future obstacles. Because we had so many individual partners with only direct financial interest in their own local company, it made it very difficult for my local partners to focus on changing the ownership and eventually the management structure to address these drawbacks.

At age 60, I implemented a transition plan, with a target to exit by 62. This turned out to be a much more difficult task than I imagined. As I mentioned earlier, the structure that I built over the years was designed for growth, and that part worked. I had not envisioned the hurdle it created to transition the firm. My original plan was to sell the original partners' shares to new partners, but it became apparent that wasn't going to work for two reasons. First, I chose to establish the values of our businesses based on a formula that was typically book value plus four times the weighted average of the preceding three years, pre-tax profit, which was designed to approximate real market values. This was in stark contrast to most of our privately held competitors, who followed shareholder agreements that valued their companies at book value. Ours worked out, in general, to value our businesses at about two times book value or an earnings multiple of about six to eight. Second, in the 20 years since I founded ERM, many larger competitors decided to go public. A few did quite well as publicly held businesses maintaining growing valuations, but most struggled, as was the case with my former employer many years before.

We had also created another obstacle to ownership transition in the form of deferred federal income taxes. As I mentioned earlier, we ran our U.S. businesses as cash-basis taxpayers. As a rapidly growing business, we deferred almost $20 million in federal and, in some cases, state taxes that would become due if we either stopped growing or, through an ownership transition, became an accrual taxpayer. For a brief time in the late 1980s, we flirted with going public. As I said earlier, a number of our competitors took that step. However, after assessing the advantages and disadvantages, and because a number of our senior partners in our affiliated companies were opposed, we dropped further consideration of that route.

10 years later, however, it became apparent that I needed to address the subject if I was ever going to monetize my interest in the firm and retire. In looking at alternatives, we decided to explore using an employee stock ownership plan (ESOP). This alternative results in the company, over time, being owned by the employees. It was thought at the time that that might be an interim move before ultimately going public.

We brought in a management consultant. We held a series of meetings with the senior partners and our consultant acting as the primary resource. The final ESOP-oriented plan was presented to the partners at a president's meeting. Following that meeting, a buying group met without me (as required) to decide whether to proceed and implement the ESOP. I remember very clearly waiting for a call that particular weekend and being very disappointed to learn that the partners turned it down. Not only did they turn it down, but they also did so with the admonition that they did not want to spend any more of their time dealing with the subject of ownership transition. They didn't want me to spend any more time on this either; rather, they wanted me to focus on continuing to grow the ERM Group.

I am not easily discouraged, although I'll admit I fell into a funk for several weeks. From my perspective, my partners just didn't seem to understand that there was no way I had to stop the clock. This problem wouldn't solve itself. The marketplace demanded a change in the way we conducted business, and I wanted to find a way to transition the ownership that benefited my partners, the business, and ultimately myself.

A few months later, at a meeting in Bermuda, our CFO, Dan Sevick; the partner overseeing our European and Asian business, Robin Bidwell; the partner overseeing our Latin American and Caribbean business, Arnon Garonzik; and I decided to take another tack. The ESOP only solved an ownership transition for the U.S.-based companies, which at that time comprised about 75 percent of the overall business. An ownership transition for the international companies required other means. We had thought a bit about what that means might be, and perhaps we could take the international companies public. We now began to pursue this avenue with more intensity. Only a couple of environmental firms were publicly held in Europe. It was clear that the financial markets in Europe had an appetite for our kind of business. We retained an investment banker to help us explore the prospect of taking just the international business public.

From the very beginning, the banker made it clear the better option was if the whole global business was taken public, as it would be more complicated to explain how part of the business was owned by the public and part was owned privately by the partners. Nevertheless, they felt it was achievable. We were just a more complicated story to tell, and it might cost us in the ultimate price per share.

I made no particular effort to keep my U.S. partners informed of this initiative, but I didn't hide it either. Eventually, my senior partners at one of our U.S. affiliates asked me about my plans. I explained what I had in mind and reminded them that they had made it very clear that they didn't want to participate, so I was proceeding without them. Somehow, that seemed to change the equation. They now decided they very much wanted to have a seat at the table. I said, "Fine. If you want to join the discussion, please do." Little by little, the U.S. partners decided that they wanted to come to this party. Meanwhile, the market conditions in the UK (we planned to launch our IPO on the London exchange) changed such that the size of the business that we could successfully launch, in the opinion of our investment bankers, grew, and we could benefit from having the greater scale of the total group. Conditions continued to change, making it more problematic that we could successfully launch an IPO even with the whole group and meet the partners' objectives to sell some of their equity, in addition to mine and my original partners. Therefore, our investment banker suggested we entertain the idea of bringing in a venture capital group as an interim step before ultimately going public. They introduced us to 3i Group, a large, publicly traded, London Stock Exchange venture capital firm, as a possible investment partner. After months of intense discussion, a price was negotiated subject to due diligence and working out many details.

This started a period of very intense internal meetings and negotiations, as all of my partners tried to maximize their share (this shouldn't have come as a surprise). Although my stake was by far the largest individual share, I was not the only partner hoping to sell. My original

ERM, Inc. partners, some of whom had already retired, still held some of their equity, and a number of my senior partners in the affiliated U.S. companies wanted to be part of the selling group. However, my original partners and I needed to make deals with each of the affiliate companies, as well as the original operating company and ERM's key senior staff. After all the arm-twisting, the original partner group relinquished approximately 15 percent of their share of the pie to the other players. This was the price, it turns out in the end, we paid for not having absolute control on the U.S. side. For the international companies, there was no such transfer, except for a special bonus to the senior executive leading that part of the group.

It was, in the end, though, a beneficial deal for the company and the shareholders, both those staying and those retiring. The company now had single ownership in all of its businesses and the capability and desire to standardize accounting practices, marketing, and strategic growth initiatives. It was a cash deal. The company's last year, which was the one that counted, turned out to be the best from an earnings standpoint that we ever experienced. Several people played significant roles in bringing this deal to a conclusion: our CFO, Dan Sevick; Robin Bidwell, who succeeded me as ERM Group CEO; our in-house legal team; and a great number of my partners, in addition to my efforts.

As an aside, several others deserve credit for ultimately making it possible to achieve this transition. One was my Young Presidents Organization (YPO) forum. I brought issues related to this ownership transition to them numerous times, asking for their input and perspective. On one occasion when I asked for their input, one of them, Harold "Spike" Yoh, who also was on the ERM Group Advisory Board, told me he was willing to help, but he doubted my resolve. Until I came firmly to that conclusion, he didn't want to hear about this particular subject. This was sobering input, and as I thought about his comments while driving back to my office, I realized that he was probably right. He said if I wanted to make this happen, he was confident I'd find a way to get it done. Somehow unconsciously, deep down in my gut, maybe the thought that I was leaving something behind, that I spent 20-plus years building this company, was keeping me from completing this transition. Then it dawned on me that I wanted to pursue other goals in my life, and I couldn't move forward without letting go of this. This bit of insight, I think, was the turning point. I recognized I wanted to go on with the next chapter in my life, rather than focus on leaving an endeavor that I found so rewarding.

Another player who should receive a lot of credit is my wife, my confidant as I struggled with some of the concessions I was being asked to make. On more than one occasion, she reminded me that my ego was getting in the way.

As part of the final negotiations with 3i, we convinced them to make an exception to their ironclad rule with respect to former owners staying around after the deal was completed. They agreed to let me serve on the new company's Board of Directors for a year. I valued that year on the board, as it allowed me to meet the new directors and participate in the initial reorientation of the business.

We accomplished the near impossible, according to our management consultant. We simultaneously replaced the founder and original management team, restructured the ownership of the business, and successfully repositioned the company for future success.

In the subsequent years, ERM refinanced five times to date. Kohlberg Kravis Roberts & Co. (KKR) is its latest financial investor, with a valuation of about $2.7 billion, plus debt. The company extended its geographical presence to over 40 countries, with 5,500 consultants, and exceeded $1 billion in net revenue. ERM is reputed to be the world's largest independent, exclusively environmental consulting firm with an emphasis on helping its clients internalize sustainability policy and practices.

In addition to this business, other chapters in my business life informed this book: COO of another publicly traded, 600-person consulting firm and an active partner in several other businesses, including a marina and a housing development company, a 15-building medical office development, several continuing care retirement communities, as well as numerous nonprofit and for-profit boards (a print and online newsletter publisher; electronic data storage, retrieval, and emergency backup; commercial banks; and laser machining of nanoscale electronics, medical, and research devices).

That is my story, yet there is so much more to share. In this book, I did my best to be honest about my triumphs and challenges while sharing my insights and experience in the hopes that you, too, will find your personal and professional successes.

If you are thinking about starting a business or jump-starting the one you have, this book provides practical advice to help you decide if that's the right move for you, and if so, how to set up, scale, and grow a successful business in any market.

— CHAPTER 1 —

BECOMING AN ENTREPRENEUR

So, you think you want to be an entrepreneur[1] and start your own business? Or perhaps take your existing business to a new plateau? If it's the former, I wrote this book to help you decide if that's the right move for you and, if it is, help you build a successful business. If it was the latter, I think you will find helpful ideas in the following chapters to become even more successful.

Before you start down what may be a pretty long road with some likely pitfalls and high hills to climb, you might want to ask yourself some basic questions, such as, "Why do I want to do this?" Is it because someone else thinks it's a good idea, or perhaps you are unable to find employment that meets your requirements and think this might be the answer? Perhaps it's a lifelong dream. Some other possibilities are the

1 The American Edition of the Oxford Dictionary and Thesaurus, Oxford University Press, 1996, defines an entrepreneur as follows: "A person who undertakes an enterprise or business, with the chance of profit or loss." This definition includes those who are self-employed, but have no other employees, to those who build businesses with tens of thousands of employees. Much of this book is intended to help those who want to build a multi-employee enterprise.

following: you can't stand your boss, you feel like you're in a dead-end job, you want more challenge, or you feel this is the best way for you to meet your economic goals.

In my case, it was a combination of some of these reasons.

I think I always wanted my own business, ever since I was a kid in grade school and junior high, shoveling snow for the neighbors, mowing lawns, and running a paper route. The actual trigger for my start in what turned out to be a very successful business, though, was being let go after 13 years, half of which I spent as the President and Chief Administrative Officer, with a publicly traded company. In hindsight, being let go, although wounding my pride, was a blessing. I was fortunate to acquire the skillset and the experience I knew would make it easier for me to build my own business at a relatively young age. I was 39 years old. My wife and I had six children, the oldest of whom was a senior in high school. We owned a beautiful home in suburbia. I had been well paid but had very little in the way of liquid savings. I enjoyed my job and felt that I was needed by the CEO and major shareholder of the company. I learned over the seven years as president that I did not see myself finishing my career with this company, as the founder and major shareholder CEO had two sons-in-law, one of whom I knew would eventually take over.

I don't know if there's a right age to start a business. One needs to have enough knowledge, energy, and, importantly, resources, and this combination comes together for different people at different times. I had numerous opportunities to work as a senior officer in other firms in my particular sector. I accepted a few interview invitations and was made some very handsome job offers. I found, in my case, that was particularly useful in helping me sort out what I wanted to do: to take the chance and start my own company. My goal was to build a successful national environmental consulting business to help industries reduce their air emissions, wastewater, and hazardous waste contributions to our environment and, in the process, create financial security for myself, my partners, and staff.

WHAT IS YOUR GOAL?

As you think about your specific circumstances, do you feel you have the necessary experience? Do you have the drive that it will take to build a business? Do others who know you well agree with your self-assessment? If you have a family, are they willing to support you, not necessarily in a monetary sense but certainly in an emotional and psychological sense? Are you and your family prepared for you to put in long hours and sustain a push for a significant number of years? Are you willing to risk your savings, and perhaps your home as may be required, to finance your business?

How would you characterize your risk profile? Are you typically risk averse, thrive on taking risks, or somewhere in the middle? Certainly, it is a risk for most in terms of the financial consequences, but it's also a risk concerning the fact that you cannot get the time back. You cannot undo the absence from your family and personal life over and beyond what would be the case with "just a job." Are you prepared to pick up the pieces if it doesn't succeed? Keep in mind that something like one out of two startup businesses is no longer in business after five years.[2] Later chapters of this book will discuss ways in which you can mitigate these risks and be one of the 50 percent that DOES make it. For now, simply think about these questions.

---

2 From a study covering 25 years by the U.S. Small Business Administration as reported by Russ Wiles in an article entitled, "Report Finds Common Traits Among Wealthy Americans" in the August 10, 2022, issue of USA Today newspaper, page 4B.

Next, make a list of the areas of expertise that you believe it will take to build your business and then honestly ask yourself how your skillset, experience, and personality line up with each of these areas. If you choose to do this exercise, share it with your spouse or partner, a family member, or a close friend, and ask them to give you some honest feedback as to whether your self-assessment is close to the person that they know. Have you thought about how you will fill in the voids where your experience and expertise or interests are not a good match?

Very few of us can honestly say when we're starting a business that we know enough about all the basic areas of building and running a successful business to carry the load by ourselves. That means that, for most, you will need to find others who can fill in where you lack the level of talent or experience needed to build a successful business. Do you have people in mind that could fill those gaps? Some missing pieces you can address with self-education—such as the basics of accounting and financial statements.

The talents required to start a successful business form a three-legged stool. It requires the technical skills required by the business, sales and marketing skills, and financial management skills. Missing a leg at startup, at a minimum, will compromise success. Many entrepreneurs have the first two skillsets but need another individual to provide the last.

There are many pluses in building a business. In spite of the risk, many entrepreneurs do succeed. A major part of the U.S. economy is built by individuals, such as yourself. There are almost 50,000,000 employees[3]

---

3 According to Drew DeSilver from the Pew Research Center in a report entitled, "10 Facts about American Workers" dated August 29, 2019, in 2014, 14.6 million people were self-employed, and they collectively employed another 29.4 million. Taken together, this represents about 30 percent of U.S. employment. A few other statistics might be of interest. In 2021, according to the U.S. Bureau of Labor and Statistics, 6,043,000 people worked for businesses that employed four or less; almost the same number worked in businesses with five to nine employees; businesses with 10 to 19 employees numbered 8,566,000; those with 20 to 49 had 12,142,000; 50 to 99 had 8,950,000; 100 to 244 had 11,462,000. In total, almost 49,000,000 people worked in businesses with fewer than 500 employees!

in small companies (under 500 employees) that were once a gleam in someone's eye.

Building a successful business can be an exhilarating, fulfilling, and rewarding experience. Under the right circumstances, the entrepreneur can create more flexibility in their schedule and, in time, achieve a reasonable work-life balance, know they had a role in giving others an opportunity to fulfill their potential, improve the world we live in, and gain financial security, among other benefits.

Another alternative for those who want to build a business with possibly less risk and which may require less experience is to purchase a startup franchise for a new business in which you are interested. There are many from which to choose. Each has a standard operating manual and, typically, continuing assistance from the franchise parent. If this appeals to you, numerous sources can provide detailed information. TIP: One of them is the International Franchise Association. This organization hosts "Open for Opportunity" roadshows in various cities in the United States. Most of the material in the rest of this book can help make your franchise succeed.

KEYS TO SUCCESS

As mentioned previously, about 50 percent of new startups, unfortunately, don't make it past the five-year mark. There are a lot of reasons for this, and often, there is more than one reason. Some of the reasons can be anticipated and mitigated. The odds of success increase when the following 11 major keys to success are addressed:

1. **Vision**—The ability to articulate what you want your business to be in five or 10 years. As an example, in my case, my vision was to build a national environmental consulting business consisting of 10 regional companies operating under the same public identity within 10 years. What is yours? Write in the margin.

2. **Passion**—Your passion to succeed makes a difference. Do you want it badly enough to make it one of the top priorities of your life? To week in and week out make the effort, do the heavy lifting, even when it requires you to sacrifice other aspects that you value?

3. **Philosophy**—For most of us, the philosophy and values we live by outside of business are likely to be the same ones we live by within our business. This holds different meanings for different people. I recall a luncheon very early in starting my business with several of my partners where we discussed our business philosophy. After a bit of a conversation, I wrote on the back of a napkin the following:

The philosophy of our company is…

Do quality work.

Produce an exceptional return.

Have fun doing it.

We tried to live by that motto. An expanded version of this, which we developed a few years later, plus our company's mission statement, can be found in Appendix 1.

4. **People**—The decisions you make in terms of who your partners are (if any), the employees you select, and having the right person in the right job (the goal of all employers) will make a material difference. The more often you get this right, the more likely you are to succeed. It is more than just a skillset; it's also the individual's attitude, values, ability to work with other people, and conflict-resolution skills. These latter items are as important, and in many cases more important, than the skillset.

5. **Culture**—Another aspect when you think about people is whether you can create a culture where the individual feels valued, treated fairly, and rewarded for their efforts. Failure at a task need not be fatal, but rather part of the learning process. Innovation is the lifeblood of a successful company. Does your attitude about people recognize that most have families and others that are important in their lives? They have other interests besides work. They want some degree of work-personal time balance in their lives (even though you may struggle to create that for yourself). To the degree that you can say yes to the above, it's been my experience that the people part of the equation works well to help you succeed.

6. **Planning**—Planning is another word for "anticipating" or thinking through where you want to go, how you're going to get there, and what you're going to need along the way. Another

word for planning is "preparation" or working hard to prepare yourself for success. Normal planning in most businesses is performed against the backdrop of a long-range (three- to five-year) strategic plan. An annual business plan includes specific goals and the steps to meet those goals in the forthcoming year. Planning for the business can be a top-down exercise, a bottom-up exercise, or some mix of the two. I tend to favor a mix of the two, but each business has to find the right balance to produce a plan that people can understand and commit to over the long haul. Keep in mind that it's usually easier to persuade people to buy in if they have a chance to *influence* that plan. Of course, in the beginning, developing your plan is primarily your job.

7. **Financing**—Many businesses fail because they are under-capitalized. It can happen in the startup phase as well as when businesses expand faster than they can support. In a later chapter, I expand on this in more detail.

8. **Sales**—As most everyone understands, if you don't have enough sales to cover your expenses, nothing else actually matters. Having an effective marketing and sales effort is crucial to your success. This is usually such an important part of any successful business that I spend some time covering this in a later chapter.

9. **Management**—You and, perhaps eventually, your management team are certainly key elements as to whether your business will succeed or fail. How quickly will you and your management team act when changes are necessary? How well do you and your employees work/play together? Are they good at putting the

company's interests first? How good are you at motivating and leading?

10. **Systems**—The systems you put in place to manage your business are critical in giving you the information you need. Is this information available to the right people when it's needed? Are the systems secure from unauthorized parties and power outages or natural disasters? Do you have a backup for all of this? There will be more on this subject later.

11. **Profitability**—The goal is to be profitable every year while still investing in growth. The key to growth and staying solvent is to produce positive cash flow—you can be profitable on paper and still run out of cash!

Finally, as honestly as you can, ask yourself the question, "Why do I believe I can build a successful business?" I suggest you write out your responses.

Whether you want to start or improve your solo physical fitness practice, a flower shop with four employees, a heating, ventilating, and air conditioning company with 150 employees, an electric bike manufacturer, or an enterprise of 66 companies with 2,500 employees in 34 countries as I did, this book was written to help you achieve your goal.

Although the bulk of my business experience was in professional services, throughout this book, I will cover most of the areas critical to the success of almost all businesses. In most cases, the topics are not covered in depth, which would fill many volumes. I encourage you to explore topics of particular interest beyond the overview provided in this book.

In the next chapter, I'll cover some of the fundamentals in launching your business.

— CHAPTER 2 —

GETTING STARTED

Presumably, you're excited or perhaps terrified, but you've decided to start your own business. There are a number of basic decisions and actions you will need to address.

What are some of the major issues that you need to consider when starting or expanding your business? Presumably, you already have the idea of what kind of service or product around which you want to build your business. That being the case, what is your sense of competition? To be one of many? In what way will you be able to successfully compete? Is it going to be on price, service, quality, unique technology, and/or convenience? What competitive advantages do you have?

A little background on how my life experiences brought me to start my own company. In my case, I graduated from Michigan State University with a master's degree in civil engineering at 24 years of age, married, and with 1.6 babies. I spent the next three years working for the Dow Chemical Company in their environmental department. Then I worked for 13 years with Roy F. Weston, Inc., now known as

Weston Solutions, Inc. This firm was one of the very earliest to provide professional environmental engineering and science services to industrial clients in the United States. Most of its clients were Fortune 500 companies in the process industries, including steel, chemical, petroleum, pulp and paper, textiles, etc. These companies dealt with increasing new state and federal regulations requiring them to address water pollution, air pollution, and solid and hazardous waste problems that previously gained minimal attention. Very few of these companies had the necessary internal expertise, even though they employed tens of thousands of employees. My prior experience with Dow Chemical Company was one of the rare firms that had extensive pollution abatement programs in place and staff to manage them.

While employed by the Weston firm, I built up a wide cadre of industry contacts in major companies throughout the United States, as well as hands-on project experience designing solutions for their industrial pollution remediation needs. Although it might seem obvious that if I started a business, it would be in that same field, instead, I spent six months with a partner, trying to acquire a local distributor for large hydraulic systems. A couple of reasons were that 1) I did not want to create a grassroots startup and 2) if acquisition candidates could be found, I would need to relocate my family and contribute possibly more capital than I could raise. As mentioned earlier, I had six children, all of whom attended public schools. Needless to say, they were not excited about moving.

I also had the experience with my former employer of starting that company's first regional office in the Midwest. It was a cold start in my seven-state regional territory. In three years, I developed enough work to employ a staff of 30 professionals. That experience gave me confidence in the skillset necessary to build a business. However, I also knew I had to commit a lot of time to make that happen as well. I hoped to find a route that wouldn't require that much time away from my family. My previous experience taught me that substantial amounts of my time would be required for a grassroots startup to succeed.

I previously looked around my region (the mid-Atlantic area) for another consulting firm that could be acquired. After exploring several possibilities, for one reason or another, that didn't seem to be a practical route. In my search for a company to buy, I found a regional 20-year-old distributorship of sophisticated hydraulic pumping systems and decided to pursue acquiring it.

Meanwhile, to feed my family and cover mortgage payments, etc., I acquired consulting assignments with three large Fortune 500 clients. Working approximately half-time, I executed the consulting work on my own, while the other half of my working hours were dedicated to acquiring the pump distributorship business. The half-time consulting assignments were financially sufficient to replace my former income. When it became apparent that the company my partner and I targeted to acquire decided that they would sell the business to the two owners' sons (which I learned, after the fact, is often a common outcome), I decided to start my own environmental consulting business. (My failure to acquire this business was a blessing in disguise!)

Your circumstances will certainly be different from mine. One of the ways you can reduce the chances that your new business will fail is by aligning your business with areas of expertise that you have already mastered. This would not have been the case for me if the acquisition attempt succeeded.

In future chapters, we will discuss other ways to build a business that do not require this much personal mastery in, for example, franchising or finding enough financial support to acquire an existing business where your expertise and experience can complement that business's core functions.

FINANCING YOUR BUSINESS

How much startup capital will you need, and where will it come from? To answer this question requires a financial plan—a startup budget with expected income and expenses on a month-by-month basis for at least a year or two. Such a budget will be based on numerous assumptions. It might help to develop three startup budgets: a worst case, most likely, and best-case scenario. Later on, there will be more discussion on developing a budget.

In my case, I was fortunate in several respects. First, service businesses are usually not capital intensive. A good rule of thumb is that personnel costs typically equal two-thirds of total costs. They don't have to carry much inventory (except as works-in-progress) and are usually paid within 30 to 60 days. I also started a business at a time when we still used fax machines and electric typewriting equipment. Second, as I mentioned previously, I already had three corporations for clients, with additional projects in the near future, providing some cash flow to start. Third, I secured a loan from a local bank where I had an established relationship. Finally, I envisioned recruiting able professionals that could help me build this business and to whom I would sell a portion of the equity of the new company. I decided to have the new company sell stock to my new partners with the proceeds of those sales retained by the company as working capital. In 1977, with me as the only employee and a few active projects, I arbitrarily set a value of $100,000 (approximately $500,000 in 2022 dollars) on the new business and decided to sell half of the company equity to future partners who provided an additional $50,000 in initial capitalization.

How do you plan to capitalize your business? This is a major roadblock for many would-be entrepreneurs. Perhaps you are fortunate enough to self-fund. If additional capital is required, other sources are partners, as in my case, investors, borrowing from family or private individuals, savings and loan entities, credit unions, loan companies, commercial banks, and online websites, such as Kickstarter and Indiegogo.

Equity investors come in many different forms, in addition to partners, family, and friends. Venture capitalists (VC) are not easily convinced to invest in startups, but it does happen. VCs is a generic term that includes individuals, small groups of individuals (think *Shark Tank*), and regional, national, and global firms such as KKR. VCs are typically a source of capital once a business has been started and is showing signs of growth and success.

Some entrepreneurs start out using their personal credit cards—this is convenient, but a very expensive source of funds. The cost of borrowed funds can vary greatly depending on the source. It pays to consider your alternatives and to pay attention to the terms and fine print before you borrow.

NAMING YOUR BUSINESS

What are you going to call your business? This, in many instances, is not a trivial issue. There are legal and marketing image issues that you should consider. If you are forming a limited liability company, you must obtain approval from the Secretary of State (in the state you intend to register).

Each state has its own criteria for an acceptable name. In making this decision, consider the following:

- Do you want the name to indicate the purpose of the business, such as Bluewater Yacht Sales?

- Do you want to attach your name or your location, such as in McDuffy's Uptown Florist? If you plan to have partners, will this impact their feelings of ownership? Will you be able to separate yourself from the business? Will it have lasting appeal and be attractive to future owners if you eventually sell your business?

- Is your choice of name memorable? Does it carry any negative connotations? Is there only one way to spell the name? Is it too long (shorter is better)?

- Is it similar to other existing businesses (this is usually one of the state's criteria for not approving a name)?

Once you select a name and register it, you may want to consider protecting it nationally by trademarking it and registering it through the U.S. Patent and Trademark Office. The registration protects the name and its artistic style. (You will probably need to retain a patent and trademark attorney to accomplish this.)

The trademark can also protect your company's logo. Most businesses adopt a graphic design as a symbol of their business and use it on all printed materials (including digital) and signage. A talented graphic artist can help you create a visually attractive and memorable logo that will project a positive image of your business. It should be sufficiently unique that it doesn't infringe on other registered marks.

Finally, if your business involves creating original intellectual property (such as software) or artistic work, you will probably want to protect it under U.S. copyright laws.

LOCATING YOUR BUSINESS

Different kinds of businesses require different location attributes. For some businesses, location can be the overriding reason for success or failure. Do your customers care where you are located? If you create a retail business or vet clinic, the answer is likely yes. If you are a software designer, for example, other factors are probably much more important.

Many startup businesses successfully launch from the entrepreneur's home (including mine), garage, shared office space, etc. Longer-term considerations—in addition to cost—usually weigh in, such as convenience for employees, access to public highways and transportation, access and cost of parking, public visibility, personal safety, quality of surrounding development, access to suppliers and customers, suitability, and so on.

Following the outbreak of the COVID-19 pandemic, many firms went completely virtual (working from home or working from anywhere), and a subset of this group now expects to remain this way, thereby eventually eliminating or greatly reducing the cost of office space, office furnishings, and utilities from the profitability equation.

During your startup phase, when costs may be a major concern, don't forget about subletting, sharing space and office equipment, or a virtual office. If you require physical office space, another way you can conserve capital is by furnishing your office with lightly used furniture, moveable partitions, and removable carpet (which you can take with you when you move!). These items can be found at a small percentage of the original cost. Try consignment stores or contact commercial realtors, who often know of businesses relocating or going out of business. Also, online sites can help locate used or free furniture, computers, printers, etc., as well as all types of display and manufacturing machinery.

KEY OUTSIDE RESOURCES

As part of your startup planning, at a minimum, you should have a commercial attorney, an accountant (with tax expertise), a commercial lender, and a commercial insurance agent as part of your initial team. In most cases, these professionals will be outside independent resources. In some cases, you, your partners, or family members may have the qualifications to fill these roles. My experience suggests that moving forward without this expertise, winging it yourself, or relying on a "free" Internet source or a well-intentioned amateur relative or friend is likely to result in a false economy.

Other outside parties that sooner or later you may want to establish a relationship with, depending on your internal needs/capabilities, might include an information technology (IT) service, human resources consulting, advertising/marketing firm, payroll service firm, and a travel agent, among others.

Do you envision your business being locally focused or regional, national, or international in scope? As I already mentioned, when I launched my company, I did so with the intent to grow a national business. I also developed a plan that I hoped would get me there. I'll share some of that later.

Certainly, one of the fundamental elements for all businesses is accounting. It's the language of business. It is an essential cornerstone in any business. It certainly helps (I argue that it is *essential*) that you, as the entrepreneur starting the business or one of your partners, have some accounting literacy. You do not need to be a certified public accountant (CPA), but you need the ability to read financial statements and understand basic accounting principles.

I encourage anyone planning to start a business, or making substantial changes in an existing business to significantly increase its growth trajectory, to seek out others to share your dreams, discuss your plans, and receive feedback. Those others can include members of your family, prospective partners, financial backers, potential customers, and yes, in selective instances, maybe a competitor or two. This is one of those cases where it pays upfront to admit you don't have all the answers and see if those you seek out can help you identify ways to strengthen your plans and reduce the inherent blind spots we all have.

All businesses maintain accounting records of sales, other forms of income, and expenses. Often, entrepreneurs start with internally prepared statements prepared by the owner or a bookkeeper, using commercially available software. Most startups transition to an outside CPA firm for at least annual financial statements. The sooner the better, from my experience.

CPAs can provide three levels of financial statements. The least comprehensive is a compilation: a basic summary of your company's finances using your data per standard accounting practice. This requires the least effort and is the least expensive. The CPA gives no assurance on the validity, conducts no tests, and makes no checks on internal controls. The CPA can, with more effort and expenses, produce a reviewed financial statement. This involves a limited examination of your records and systems, enough to vouch that your financial statements are free from any material misstatements and meet generally accepted accounting principles. If needed, your CPA can produce a fully audited financial statement. This entails a greater involvement and cost. They conduct certain tests, perform a thorough review, and perhaps interview some of your staff. Lenders usually want at least an independent CPA-prepared reviewed statement. A discussion with your CPA will give you further insight into the differences and help you decide which would be best for your business. If you start with a compiled statement, as you grow, it may be desirable or necessary to change to a reviewed or audited financial statement.

The next big question you should ask is: *What is the best option for legally organizing my business?* The common options are covered in the next chapter.

— CHAPTER 3 —

DEALING WITH LEGAL ORGANIZATIONAL FORMS AND TAXES

You will have three basic decisions to make when you launch a new business. What legal form will it take? Second, depending on your response to the first, you may have a choice of being a cash or accrual taxpayer. Finally, you may have the choice of setting the business tax year as other than the calendar year.

We'll deal with the first element. The simplest form of legal organization is called a proprietorship. This is where an individual and the business are synonymous concerning legal liability, as well as taxes.

Some businesses are organized as a partnership. This form does not provide partners a personal liability shield either. A mutation of the latter is a partnership with limited liability and is noted in the entity name, such as the Nancy Sisters Partnership, L.P. All forms of partnership are passthrough entities, which means their business income (or loss) is passed through to the partners responsible for payment along with their personal income tax return.

In most instances, entrepreneurs want to protect their personal assets from liabilities that originate from their business. There are several other legal structures that offer this protection. One is a limited liability company (LLC). Often, entrepreneurs start as proprietorships and then convert to a single-member LLC.

If a business is established as a regular limited liability corporation, the name of the business reflects that as ABC Company, Inc. or Incorporated. There are a couple of possible forms of corporations, depending on your type of business, the number of equity holders, and the state in which you are incorporated.

Federal law allows a limited liability corporation or Inc., if qualified, to elect to be classified as a subchapter S corporation, referring to a chapter in the Internal Revenue Code. There are several major differences between subchapter S corporations and regular so-called "C" corporations (C again represents a chapter in the Internal Revenue Code). In general, subchapter S-type corporations are treated, for federal tax purposes, like partnerships with the income of the corporation allocated to the shareholders in proportion to their individual ownership interests. The shareholders then pay income taxes on the allocated income at their ordinary income tax rate. With a C corporation, the corporate tax liability is paid directly by the corporation. All but a few states (Alaska, Florida, Nevada, New Hampshire—with exceptions for investment income, South Dakota, Tennessee, Texas, Washington, and Wyoming) also tax corporate income, and many local jurisdictions also have income taxes. Many states that tax corporate income also permit federal subchapter S corporations to make a similar election at the state level. Suffice it to say that income tax consideration is one of the significant items to consider in terms of how and where you organize your company.

It is possible, in some circumstances, to start in one form and migrate to another as time passes. It's not necessarily a decision you have to make and live with for the rest of your business life.

In many cases, it may be preferable to start as a proprietorship or partnership and, as the business grows and experiences a successful trajectory, convert to a limited liability entity. It costs little to set up a limited liability corporation, but it takes time and money to close it, should the business itself close. State and federal laws and regulations governing business legal structures and taxes have changed over time and will likely continue to do so. Competent business attorneys and tax accountants can outline your options and help you select the best option for you.

Each business is set up under state law, not federal. Therefore, the state in which you set up or register dictates specific requirements. You do not have to necessarily incorporate or register your business in the state in which you are domiciled (where your principal office is located). There may be advantages to setting up your business in a state other than where you live or where your business is located. In any case, you should register your company with the secretary of state in every state in which you expect to do more than a *de minimis* amount of business. Each form of ownership has benefits and disadvantages. State law may limit the options available to you. For instance, some states will not allow professional service firms offering engineering, architectural, or legal services to form limited liability entities.

I am not qualified to give you either legal or tax advice. My intent is simply to outline basic choices and options available to you. I strongly encourage you to seek guidance from a qualified attorney and tax accountant to see which form of ownership works best for you.

TAXES

Continuing with the discussion of taxes, it is important to become familiar with the kind of taxes that you will face. Depending on the kind of business you set up and the state or locality, you may or may not be required to collect sales taxes. If you're selling in more than one state, each state has its own ground rules relative to that which is taxed.

If your business will import or export component materials, you will need to verify the kind of tariffs or duties to which you may be subject.

Depending on the legal form you choose for your business and the type of business, you may have the choice of paying your taxes on a cash basis. That's the same basis you and I as individuals pay our individual income taxes. For some businesses, there's an advantage to being a cash-basis taxpayer, particularly for a growing business. (Cash basis means your tax obligation is based on net income as determined by subtracting actually *paid* expenses from funds *received* from sales.) Simply put, the cash basis allows the business to recognize income and expense the same way you recognize income and expense when managing your personal checkbook. If your business expenses are typically paid before you receive payment from your customer, being a cash-basis taxpayer can reduce your taxes temporarily (which, in my case, was over 20 years until the business was recapitalized). That difference in timing is a free working capital loan from the government, but of course, this will catch up with you if you have a year in which the reverse happens, such that your business shrinks or some other unusual event causes your cash income to exceed your cash expenses. However, in that case, you should be okay because you will receive the cash with which to pay your taxes. You can legally "manage" your cash profit to a degree by timing invoices such that you receive payment in the next tax year. This has the consequence of increasing the future year's cash income and decreasing working capital. "C" corporations are typically required to pay taxes on an accrual basis,[4] where your income is determined by the difference between the income you are *entitled* to receive from sales, less expenses that you *paid or are contractually obligated to pay* relative to that income. If you're growing a business, that means you're going to pay more income tax than you would otherwise if you were on a cash basis.

Your tax year doesn't necessarily have to be the calendar year—again, depending on the type of business, legal structure, etc. Your attorney or tax accountant can help you evaluate whether you are eligible for a non-calendar tax year and if it is beneficial. A potential advantage for shifting your tax year could include better alignment with your business's cash flow. Another is to offset your annual planning and budgeting cycle from the end-of-calendar-year holidays when staff like to take extra vacation time.

SHAREHOLDER AGREEMENTS

If you plan to bring in partners to start your business or as your business grows, having a shareholder agreement in writing is critical to avoid potential misunderstandings and complications later. Shareholder agreements can address the ownership the individual shareholders acquire, as well as a myriad of other considerations, including the following:

4 Professional service corporations (a subset of chapter C corporations) may qualify to be cash-basis taxpayers.

- Under what circumstances can shareholders sell equity and to whom?
- What happens if a shareholder leaves the business?
- What happens to shareholders' equity if they are disabled or, as one of my partners used to say, suffer a "TUD" (tragic and untimely death)?
- If the equity is co-owned by non-employed individuals, what happens if there is a separation of the parties?
- Does the company have a right, or obligation, to buy the stock back?
- How is the equity valued?
- Can a shareholder be required to contribute additional capital?
- Can their interests be diluted through the sale of future shares?

If you feel it's necessary to protect the business from competition that may originate from former shareholders, the shareholder agreement should address this topic.

No law requires you to use an attorney; however, with so many ways to go wrong in putting one of these documents together, you would be well advised to find a good commercial attorney with experience in this arena to assist you. See Appendix 2 for a Table of Contents from a shareholder agreement that was drafted by our corporate counsel in consultation with myself and my initial partners. This agreement is not intended or suggested to be an appropriate one for your particular business; it is purely for reference. For 20 years and eventually 150-plus partners in 66 companies, the shareholder agreements did not deviate in any substantial way from the original agreement. I also never had a single shareholder-related conflict with my partners. If you have a shareholder agreement with required company repurchase in the event of a death or permanent disability, it may be prudent for the company to buy "key man" life and disability insurance to cover the potential financial risk to the company. Lenders also like this as it reduces their risk.

The next critical step, if not already taken, is to develop your business plan. The next chapter outlines some of the key elements that should be addressed.

— CHAPTER 4 —

CRAFTING A BUSINESS PLAN

The previous chapters addressed several topics that you should consider as you start your own business. Now it's time to pull this all together into a business plan. Before you start drafting your plan, think about your target audience. Your business plan is an invaluable tool whether you plan to use it for personal use or to share it with friends, family, potential partners, investors, a commercial lender, or others who might help finance your venture. Are the documents you plan to prepare tailored to the intended audience? Most seasoned entrepreneurs encourage you not to skip this step. If you find putting this plan together very difficult, then you probably need to do more homework before actually launching your business. Every business plan has at least five basic elements:

- **Customer**. What is your service or product? Who is the client/customer, and what is the size of your market? How and why will they buy?

- **Competition**. What does your competition look like?

- **Talent**. What human talent is needed, and what evidence do you have that you have or can attract the skills and experience you will need?

- **Assets**. What physical or intellectual assets are needed?

- **Financing**. What is your projected profit or loss for at least the first 12 months? How much outside capital will you need, where is it coming from, and how will you allocate it?

The first is fairly straightforward. Do you have any marketing information where you can quantify your expected customers? Be specific. If you can identify any by name, do so. Where are your customers located? What are the demographics of your potential customers? How big is your potential market?

How will you find your customers, and how will they find you? In brief, what is your marketing plan to identify, reach, and motivate your customers to buy? What is the plan to sell your product or service?

Regarding competition, how many competitors do you have? How do you expect to compete against your competition?

When you address talent, how do your background and qualifications pertain to your new business? Do you have partners and, if so, what roles will they play and what are their qualifications for those roles? What is your organizational structure going to look like in the beginning and down the road and who will fill those key posts? (You will probably wear several hats and utilize outside parties or part-time help at the start.) What relevant experience and qualifications do they have for those jobs? How do you plan to find the people that you will need to staff your new business?

Considering assets, it is important to identify the major assets that you require in the near future, such as equipment, facilities, software (if a significant cost), warehouse space, etc.

Financing, as mentioned in Chapter 2, at this stage, you should include a budget that at least covers the first 12 months of operations, showing expected income and expenses broken down with sufficient detail to depict a high-definition picture for others of what you expect for your first year. Typically, it is much easier to forecast your expenses than your income, so it may be particularly helpful to you and those who help finance your business to prepare three budgets: an optimistic (best-case) version, a worst-case one, and a third, perhaps the most realistic.

When preparing to finance your business, it's best to assume the worst-case scenario, plus a cushion, because happy surprises are usually not a problem. State what you need in financing assistance, spell out where you will allocate additional funds, and identify how and when you expect to pay it back. Be prepared to discuss what you can offer to securitize a loan. When going through this exercise, try to be as realistic as possible. Try hard to nail down all of the expenses you likely will incur. If possible, avoid long-term commitments, even if they cost more in the short run. If your business take off doesn't work or is much slower than your finances can support, shorter commitments yield a shallower financial hole.

DEVELOPING A BUDGET

A useful exercise is to isolate your expenses into two categories: fixed and variable. Particularly when you're first starting your business, try to minimize fixed costs. Fixed costs are reasonably independent of your sales in the first year, such as rent, utilities, insurance, and other costs not associated with producing your product or service. A variable cost is directly associated with providing the service or product, such as the materials, transportation, labor, etc.

Next, calculate your potential gross profit and gross margin by subtracting your variable costs from your sales budget (projected gross income). As a hypothetical example, let's assume, in the first year, your budgeted variable costs are $300,000 to support your sales budget of $500,000. Then your projected gross profit will be $200,000, and the resulting gross margin will equal 40 percent ($200,000/$500,000). Your break-even point is determined by dividing your fixed cost (in this case, I assumed) of $180,000 (again, from your budget) by the gross margin. In this example, your break-even sales would equal $450,000. If you generate $500,000 in sales income, your budgeted profit is $50,000. Until you reach $450,000 in sales income, you will operate at a loss. To make matters worse, it's likely you will pay expenses before you receive cash for your product or service, making your cash loss even greater.

Business Expenses and Categories for a Typical Startup

- Advertising
- Bank service charges
- Business development/sales expenses/trade shows, etc.
- Cleaning and janitorial services
- Contributions
- Equipment leasing
- Fringe benefits
- Furnishings lease
- Hospitality/entertaining (customers, suppliers, employees, etc.)
- Insurance (property, casualty, auto, liability, etc.)
- Internet
- IT support (outside resource)
- Licenses and permits
- Maintenance of building and grounds
- Material cost of goods sold
- Membership/dues
- Maintenance of equipment
- Miscellaneous
- Office supplies (including software and stationery)
- Outside service contracts
- Payroll taxes
- Professional services (legal, accounting, etc.)
- Property/office space lease
- Recruiting/pre-employment expenses
- Salary or wages
- Shipping
- Signage
- Subcontracts (other)
- Subscriptions
- Taxes other than payroll and income (sales, excise, VAT, occupational)
- Telephone (mobile and fixed)
- Travel
- Utilities
- Vehicle leases
- Vehicle operation, maintenance, and registration fees

This is certainly not necessarily an all-inclusive list; some of these cost categories may not apply to your business, and your particular niche may have some unique expenses that are not listed.

In the next chapter, I'll cover the people part of your plan. For many businesses, staff can be 60 to 70 percent of total costs. Besides the financial impact, staffing is one of and, maybe for your business, the *key* to your current and future success.

— CHAPTER 5 —

FINDING AND KEEPING EMPLOYEES

The people you select and who join your business are most likely going to have a major effect on your success, or lack thereof. Selecting people you want and need to build your business is one of the most important tasks for an entrepreneur building a successful business. In the beginning, you will likely be the decision maker, and as such, you will find that locating, hiring, and motivating people is part art and part science. There is an abundance of advice in a myriad of publications from academics, human resource professionals, and psychologists, offering ideas and tools to evaluate people through psychological profiles, their aptitudes, and interests to help with screening applicants and selecting whom you hope will be the winners. Past performance and references, among others, are evidential tools, but in the end, a great deal of any personnel decision comes down to your perceptions of the individual's personality, value system, drive, and willingness to take constructive criticism and be a team player—that's where the art part comes into play.

If your business requires personnel with substantial expertise or on-the-job training, turnover of your personnel can be very expensive. You want to avoid a revolving door, constantly hiring people only to see them leave after a short time, particularly if you have selected good people in the first place.

There are many factors to the decision that employees make every day to come to work again, rather than seek employment at a different company. What is their sense of commitment? What actions will you take to help your employees grow in their careers? The more they sense your commitment to their success, the more likely they will commit to the business's success.

As previously discussed, the culture in your company is one of the major factors that attracts and keeps people. Do people feel empowered? Do they feel appreciated for the jobs they perform? Do they feel fairly compensated? Do they feel encouraged to take reasonable risks and that failure is just a part of the learning process? Do they buy into the win-win attitude with coworkers, or are they of the zero-sum mindset—if you win, I lose? Do they feel motivated to improve and adopt a strong work ethic? Are they rewarded for exceeding expectations? Do they feel generally in the "know" regarding business operations and updates? Is being a mentor and mentoring others encouraged?

Employees tend to stay with businesses if, when asked, they can say "yes" to most of these questions. There is a long list of other items that influence people's desires to stay, such as changing family circumstances and the company's willingness or ability to demonstrate some flexibility when employees need it.

Inevitably, as time passes, sooner or later, some personnel will no longer pull their weight, reduce or sabotage the effectiveness of others, or simply not get along with other employees. A company's response to these individuals also affects your other employees' decision to stay with your business or leave. Oftentimes, the boss is the last one to know if there is an employee hurting productivity and/or morale. Do your best to try to identify these situations before they become obvious to everyone. Identify the root cause. Is the problem fixable with training, coaching, or counseling to remedy it? Sometimes, an effort to move that employee within the company to another job or another setting can work for everyone. When none of the above is practical or effective, then separating the individual as humanely as possible is in everyone's best interest. Although, presumably, most of the actions you take are between you and the individual employee, rest assured, if there are other employees, they generally note how you handle the situation. You want your actions to be a plus, not a minus for your other employees. Your image as an employer is enhanced when you terminate an employee showing respect for the individual, compassion (as appropriate), fairness, and firmness.

The best guidance I can give for terminating employees is to follow the golden rule. Arrange a private setting at the end of the workday, preferably also the end of the workweek. This allows the individual as much privacy as possible. If you think there is a possible legal repercussion from this termination—age, disability, gender, or race discrimination issues—obtain human resources and legal advice and follow it. If not, to the extent you can, be truthful in telling them why they are terminated. Explain the expectations of them going forward—returning company property; filling out required paperwork; communicating, as needed, with customers, suppliers, and other employees—as well as what they can expect from the company—severance pay, if any; benefit coverage; arrangements for returning personal property; unemployment insurance coverage; potential reference requests from future employment prospects; and their alternatives if they participate in a company retirement plan. If there is a noncompete agreement in place, review the restrictions and advise if the company intends to enforce it. It helps if all of these elements are documented in writing (again, if legal action is a possibility, have it reviewed by legal counsel first). This is naturally a stressful encounter for both parties. Putting the essentials in writing helps reduce the inaccuracy of memories.

When terminating personnel, try to show your respect for the individual and value for him/her as a person. If you can honestly provide positives relative to their employment, do so. A little empathy can go a long way.

I recall a case that may illustrate what *not* to do. The regional manager of a previous employer decided to terminate a branch office manager. He arrived unannounced, walked into his office, and told him he was terminated immediately. He stood there as the office manager, as he directed, emptied his personal items into a box, collected his office keys, and walked him to his company car. Meanwhile, others in the office were active spectators. When the regional manager arrived at the employee's residence, he dropped off the employee and his box of possessions and drove away.

The next day, I received a call from the former branch manager's wife. She was understandably irate that her husband was treated so insensitively. I agreed with her and apologized on behalf of the company. Then, I called the regional manager and confirmed the way the termination occurred. I asked why he handled it that way, and he explained that he didn't want any company files or property to be removed by the manager, particularly relative to new business opportunities. When we finished the conversation, I was assured that there would never be a repeat performance.

To keep people and keep them motivated, give employees constructive feedback on a regular basis. This is a routine practice in companies that retain quality employees. This is good practice, even for startups. The staff wants to know where they stand; they want to know whether they meet or exceed expectations. If not, they want to know why not.

Feedback loops work best when they work both ways. Feedback is also a tool to give supervisors, including yourself, input from employees. We all have blind spots, and this is a tool that can reduce them.

Performance reviews should occur regularly, whether every six months or a year, as well as spontaneous kudos when staff members achieve goals. It helps people know they are appreciated. When issues arise, constructive criticism, along with necessary steps for success the next time, helps boost morale. Employees usually know if they missed the mark and suspect that you know, too. A conversation can be helpful in improving the odds of success in the future. Psychologists say, for most people, it takes about six positive feedback loops to balance one negative.[5] Therefore, it's very important when addressing performance that you look honestly for areas where praise is appropriate.

Some employers prefer to conduct performance reviews for all employees at the same time—perhaps the month of June or December. The advantage of this practice is that all employees receive the benefit or the reverse of the company's performance and the general business conditions at the same time. If salary adjustments follow performance reviews, this offers the perception of fair, equal treatment. Such adjustments also can coincide with your budget year, which can correlate to a bonus or incentive compensation plan. The major downside of all of this feedback and compensation consideration at once is overloading

---

5 Jack Zenger and Joseph Falkman, "The Ideal Praise-to-Criticism Ratio," Harvard Business Review, March 15, 2013.

your business with this administrative effort all at the same time. Also, if compensation changes are made at this time, your labor costs increase all at once, instead of incrementally. The other common time for performance reviews is on or near the employee's employment anniversary. In this case, care should be taken not to let a particularly good or bad month overly influence reviews and changes in compensation.

Turnover in your business is an important indicator of your hiring practices, the culture you create, and the way you treat people.

LOCATING PROSPECTIVE EMPLOYEES

Finding employees in normal times is usually not the challenge; it's finding the *right* employees. Many entrepreneurs find, in the startup mode, they can find the people they need from past employment associations—individuals that they worked with in the past with the requisite skills. These people are always a lower risk than hiring people with whom you don't have actual working experience. Another avenue is to ask existing employees, family, friends, or former associates for references to individuals for potential hire. The online site LinkedIn is another source of finding talent. There are still "want ads" in news publications (even though they are a vanishing breed, they still exist and can still produce results). Additional possibilities include other online sites, such as indeed.com, or direct communication with trade and professional organizations. In some cases, local trade schools, college placement offices, or job fairs yield results. Although it's unlikely to be necessary at this stage, you might one day need to resort to personnel search firms. These suggestions are applicable mostly to high-skilled positions. In some cases, social media can be fruitful in identifying candidates.

For seeking unskilled or semi-skilled individuals, help wanted signage may be useful. Sometimes, temporary help agencies can meet the need.

Employers often overstate the minimum qualifications an applicant must have for consideration, for instance, requiring five years of related experience when one or two years is sufficient. Many businesses require a college degree for positions that, in reality, don't require a degree. Setting unnecessary minimum qualifications for applicants reduces the pool of possible candidates.

Once candidates are identified, reviewing résumés and applications is the usual next step. If you find individuals who, on paper (or the computer screen), demonstrate potential, you might consider screening them further with a telephone interview or, better yet, Zoom or a similar app. If your instincts tell you the candidate could be a fit, the next step is to check references. Listen carefully to what the reference does NOT say, as well as what they DO say, keeping in mind that references are selected by the candidate and likely will only provide you the positives. Also, former employers may have liability concerns. If a former employer claims a company policy not to provide references, it may indicate they have nothing good to say about your candidate. If circumstances permit, identify other people beyond the references who know this individual. You should ask the candidate if they mind if you contact other individuals.

When hiring for key positions, there is no substitute for in-person interviews. Sometimes it takes more than one to make you comfortable to make an informed decision. I found it helpful to urge candidates during an interview to be as honest as possible, recognizing that they too do not want to make the wrong decision. If it turns out not to be a good fit, both you and the candidate suffer a loss.

In some instances, for key positions, consider meeting the employee and their spouse or partner. More often than not, the spouse or significant other will influence your prospective employee's decision to join your business, as well as stay with the company once hired. In these cases, it's especially important that the spouse/partner has an opportunity directly to learn who you are and what working for your business will be like. It also gives you another chance to see your prospective employee's actions in a different setting. This often gives you a sense of their spouse/partner's wants. This may be very helpful in influencing the terms and content of your offer, assuming you decide to hire this individual.

A word of caution in selecting or promoting employees: we all bring our personal biases into the decision. My experience suggests that good-looking people are hired over those whom we think are less attractive. Tall people receive the nod over shorter folks, even when they are not the most qualified. Men are often selected over more qualified women. Race can also play a role. I worked for a firm where my impression was, more times than not, senior management gave extra weight to those who were attractive and tall. Other factors that unconsciously weigh on our selection process might include the individual's heritage, taste in music and books, etc. Rarely does this help in finding the best person for your business. Remember, you want to avoid any complaints regarding the candidate interviewing process based on violation of an anti-discrimination law.

Entrepreneurs have found testing tools they believe help them select those they wish to hire. Some of these are in the public domain and can be found in an Internet search. One such test is the Myers-Briggs Personality Test. I found this test to be very helpful, not only as a tool in selecting people but to aid the existing management team in better understanding each other. We are all "wired" differently in the way we respond to others and our everyday world. The Myers-Briggs test provides insight into how each of us functions, thinks, and responds in different business and personal situations.

If, at this stage, you already hired a few key employees, consider having them interview your prospects and report back their views on who will make the best fit. We all see people and situations differently, and this is certainly a case where two heads are better than one. Another advantage of obtaining input from existing employees is they will feel they had a say in who is hired and with whom they will work. This results in improving communications and teamwork.

Some of the characteristics I found in top performers I hired include:

- Intelligence
- Can-do attitude
- Ambitious; strong drive to succeed
- Good work ethic
- Flexible
- Good "people sense"
- Emphasis on what they can do for the business, rather than the reverse
- Strong desire for self-improvement and self-empowerment
- Willing to share with others
- Empathy

As an extreme example of several of these characteristics, a friend of mine was en route, by train, from Washington, DC, to Philadelphia to deliver a presentation to a senior executive of a Fortune 100 company. He finally succeeded in scheduling this appointment after numerous attempts. The train stopped on a stretch of tracks near Baltimore. The conductor advised there was a power outage (electric-driven train), and they didn't know when power would be restored. He grabbed his presentation, exited the train (over the conductor's strenuous objection), climbed over a fence while dressed in a suit and tie, made his way to a street in this depressed neighborhood, hailed a private car (long before Uber), and convinced the driver to take him 85 miles north to Philadelphia. He made his appointment on time, gave the presentation, and won a large consulting assignment. I certainly wouldn't hold this up to my staff as an example of what I'd expect of them.

MAKING THE HIRE

Once you find the right hire, the next challenge is to find the right combination of compensation and non-economic considerations acceptable to both you and the candidate. Seldom, if ever, is compensation a secret among your employees. The best practice is to be fair to others already in your employment, as well as the new hire. Again, consider non-financial considerations (more on this subject later) that many employees value and offer a benefits package that both parties can accept.

CONTRACT EMPLOYEES

Many companies, including startups, hire workers classified as contract employees. Legally, these workers must remain truly independent. As such, the company does not incur payroll taxes, cover employee benefits, or address certain employee-employer responsibilities like safety and health. These advantages often tempt employers to treat workers as contract employees when they are not. These poor business practices expose the company to hefty fines and penalties, in addition to paying the avoided taxes, and have put some companies out of business. Be forewarned. If in doubt, obtain legal advice from a labor attorney.

SELECTING THE BEST

As mentioned previously, every business has its own culture. In the beginning, the entrepreneur consciously or unconsciously establishes the culture of the business. Successful businesses typically foster a culture that attracts, motivates, and keeps the productive employees. It's a cycle that feeds on itself. It gives value to its customers and seems to maximize profitability over the long run.

As an employer, you try to derive the highest sustainable productivity from the employees you hire. My experience suggests a policy of finding the highest-quality individual for a particular job. Paying above market in salary and benefits pays off in productivity, less turnover, and higher morale. Each type of business has its own competitive employment environment, but with that caveat, I found maintaining compensation for all employees at the 75th percentile, relative to comparable employment opportunities, pays a big dividend in the long run. Data on compensation can be found, depending on your business sector, on government sites, professional and trade associations, compensation firms, etc. I encourage you to find the very best talent you can afford because they cost less in the long run. Studies show the difference in productivity between outstanding versus average employees can equal as much as five times.[6] Hire the smartest and most motivated folks you can attract—they come in all sizes, shapes, genders, ages, and colors.

---

6 Berta Aldrich, *Winning the Talent Shift,* John Wiley & Sons, Inc., 2021

Another category of potential employees is "older" people—say over 50 years old. Many employers are reluctant to hire older people due to the perception that they may be technically out of date, slower to accept new ways, likely to have more health insurance claims, etc. In some cases, these negatives are valid. Offsetting pluses, however, may include seasoning and experience that you can leverage, the likelihood of perhaps fewer family distractions, a better work ethic than younger folks, and sometimes a willingness and ability to make great mentors.

Two short examples from my experience are as follows. As a 28-year-old regional manager, I needed to hire someone to help me build and deliver an engineering design service. George, the candidate I was fortunate to hire, was 25-plus years my senior. He had built an engineering design firm and sold it when his doctor told him he had cancer and only six months to live. Happily, his doctor's diagnosis turned out to be wrong. However, having sold his own business, he was looking for a job. George succeeded in building the design team for me, and he proved to be a great mentor in sharing his experience in building his own business.

In another case, a couple years after I started my business, I hired Eleanor, a woman in her early seventies who retired twice before, to oversee office supplies and our copy center and to generally help wherever needed. She later became our receptionist and continued to work for us into her early nineties. One winter, the weather service predicted a heavy snowfall starting in the early evening. Without anyone asking her to do so, Eleanor checked into a nearby hotel. The next morning, she had someone at the hotel drive her to our office in spite of only one lane out of four on the highway leading to our office being plowed. She was at her receptionist desk before 8 a.m. when the calls started coming in from our much younger staff. When they heard her voice instead of the expected voicemail, they had a hard time explaining that they wouldn't be in because of the storm. That's dedication personified.

COMPENSATION AND CULTURE

From my experience, when considering your compensation strategy, what you pay individuals is *not likely to be a secret.* Sooner or later, your employees generally figure out what other people make. Do your best to make it fair and pay people well for the job they perform, regardless of race, gender, or previous salaries. Following these guidelines attracts and keeps good people and reduces turnover, which saves money. Best of all, you can hold your head up when you look in the mirror knowing you treated people right. Ideally, the compensation system needs to be seen as fair by your employees. It's also important to recognize compensation is only part of valuing and motivating people to succeed in their jobs.

There are numerous other factors that play into employee satisfaction. One of them is whether they feel recognized when a job is well done. Be quick to praise publicly and slow to criticize—and then only privately and as constructively and fairly as possible. Other non-monetary aspects that employees often value include a company's culture and its willingness to be flexible, a setting that makes them feel respected and their work valued, one that keeps them informed on issues that matter to them, one that conveys the message that management is interested in them, one that helps them develop their potential, and one that listens and responds to their ideas and concerns. It all matters.

The culture of the business can mean a great deal. Is it family-friendly? Do your supervisors understand that people have a life outside of work, which at times can be very stressful? Recognizing their individual circumstances sends people the message that you, and the organization, care. Family leave time, when needed, can be an important perk. Some of us are solar-powered, so outside light for people required to work inside can be highly valued. Another way to say "I really care" and improve productivity is through a fair way to resolve grievances. Encourage employees to suggest ways to improve your product, service, or working conditions, and then respond to those ideas. Do you accommodate people with special needs? All these elements add up to a culture that increases the odds of a successful business.

JOB DESCRIPTIONS AND TITLES

For most businesses starting from scratch, job descriptions are usually a low priority. Startups look to hire people with a can-do attitude and who will do whatever is required. The job often consists of a little bit of this and a little bit of that, and often, as the business grows, they will ultimately become separate jobs. Recognize that some people are uncomfortable with positions that lack (from their point of view) structure. This is another area to explore when you hire people, particularly early in your company's existence. As your business grows, however, it will become increasingly important to make sure each individual has a clear understanding of the tasks for which they are responsible, partly to ensure a lack of confusion and any gaps in coverage. It's a bit of an art form to craft job descriptions that are unambiguous and accurately cover jobs, duties, authority, and responsibilities. If this is not in your particular skillset, by the time the business grows in size to where this is important, you should consult someone with professional human resources experience to assist with or fulfill this task. You can also outsource this function to consulting firms when you need it.

Job titles, in my experience, are best used sparingly and only when necessary. Titles are important to people. It may be tempting as you start out to generously hand out titles. Once given, they are very hard labels to take away without losing the individual. If the person you hire fulfills the role of general manager, vice president, or department head in a small organization, they may or may not be the person you need in that role as the company grows. If they are not, but they are otherwise a good, productive employee, you could potentially lose that individual by stripping away their title, which they will view as a demotion, or continue to work with someone who is no longer qualified to fulfill that job. Sometimes, the nature of your business makes a strong job title critical, particularly with employees who work directly with customers. As a generality, it matters how customers feel when they communicate with a designated senior person in the firm. Semantics—the words with which you label a person, place, or object—have practical implications. That's why you seldom see a "used car" lot; rather, "previously owned" cars are sold on the premises. The person selling the product is not a salesperson, but an associate. Be creative in this sense with titles that make your customer feel they receive special attention from staff while also not causing future internal titling problems. At ERM, Inc., in our early years, we did not use the title vice president; we adopted titles such as principal, and, later, associate, indicating only that they were owners. As our staff numbers grew, we too had to expand titles along functional lines, i.e., Project Manager, Project Scientist, etc. Another potential drawback to titles is giving some employees too limited a view of their job, resulting in "that's not my job" mindset. This can be seen in small things, like staff walking by trash near the front door and not feeling they should pick it up, to major things, like seeing a quality issue and feeling someone else is responsible to flag or fix it.

FRINGE BENEFITS AND TOTAL AWARDS

Employees and potential employees are almost universally concerned with benefits. Fringe benefits, for employers, are a significant cost and an effective tool in attracting and keeping employees. It's usually a particularly difficult pill to swallow for entrepreneurs starting a new business. However, as stated earlier, benefits, depending on your type of business, can be exceedingly important in attracting and keeping good people. I will continue to reiterate this theme over and over that it's good people, *exceptional* people, that increase the odds of you building a successful business. The usual list of benefits that employers offer includes medical and hospitalization insurance and might include dental and eye care, paid vacation, paid sick leave, personal time off to care for family members, a retirement plan, continuing education support, and life insurance, as well as death, dismemberment, and disability insurance. In some cases, they might include free parking, public transportation vouchers, employment opportunities for employees' children, contributions to a scholarship fund for employees' children, or membership in a health club or an onsite exercise facility (providing a coffee/snack space is almost universally valued—even better if the business provides it for free), and the list could go on. Not every prospective employee or current employee values each of these fringe benefits equally. As an example, for some, health care coverage is crucial, but to others, it matters very little as they have coverage under a spouse's or partner's plan. After medical insurance, the most expensive benefit usually involves time off with pay, but sometimes, that is THE most important benefit to an employee.

To some, the ability to take time off, even without pay, upon proper notice or the flexibility to work from home is a highly valued perk. It's hard to imagine an entrepreneur in a startup position selecting more than a few benefits from this list, so make the ones you select count from your employees' perspective. You will also want to consider the benefits that your competition offers when assembling an affordable plan. Once employees are provided a benefit, it is very difficult to reduce or eliminate it.

Strange as it may seem, you might want to consider a four-day workweek. This is an old idea currently being adopted by companies in a number of industries. The concept is to produce more in less time—four eight- or nine-hour days as well as reformatting the 40-hour standard work week with 10-hour days. A four-day week might be a very valuable recruiting and retention tool. Large firms, such as Panasonic and Microsoft, have tried it and claim that productivity increased.[7] Several governments have tried it as well, such as Iceland. If you want to explore this more, I encourage you to contact 4 Day Week Global, a nonprofit that helps companies implement four-day workweek programs around the world. This could give you a competitive advantage in attracting and retaining employees.

ACCOMMODATIONS AND WORKSPACE

If your business requires accommodating employees in offices or other indoor spaces, you may want to consider the implications of making provisions for your employees. Before I offer some suggestions in this

7 Gene Marks, "The Argument for a Four-Day Work Week," The Philadelphia Inquirer p. A10, March 3, 2020.

regard, let me say that for most startup companies, the kind and quality of workspace is usually not a major consideration for employees. The space you need to operate your business can be expensive, and most employees recognize this. On the other hand, though, the amount and quality of space affects morale and productivity. With office-based businesses, if people are jammed into tight quarters with a lack of privacy, one employee's activity often reduces the concentration and execution of job responsibilities of the other employees around them. There are ways around this, for instance, by having designated spaces available for people who need to make phone calls or hold meetings with others. As mentioned previously, most people respond to light, airy, clean, pleasingly decorated space. Each business makes decisions as to appropriate tradeoffs for improved productivity, higher morale, and improved ability to attract and keep people with the cost of space. Sometimes, people equate their value to the company by the size or location of their office or workspace. It's best to keep that in mind when assigning space to your employees. Travel time and cost, safety of the area, proximity to other amenities (parking, gyms, restaurants, public transportation, airport, shopping, etc.) are some other factors that employees consider.

The COVID-19 pandemic that began in early 2020 permanently shifted some employees' work location, in many cases, to their homes. This can be a significant plus for employees, but remote work locations present additional challenges to monitor productivity, maintain your culture, and create teamwork.

CONTINUING EDUCATION AND TRAINING

Most employees value company-sponsored training complementary to their goals that also often provides additional advancement opportunities. It can be a relatively inexpensive endeavor for the company and will often make a difference in bringing the kind of people you want aboard, keeping them, and building their knowledge and skills as an add-on to their regular job experience. Depending on your business, encouraging people to belong to and take an active role in their professional or trade association might be a plus for both the business and the employees. Many businesses implement policies that provide financial incentives for employees that obtain additional certifications or licenses. Other training and skill-building tools include online training resources, trade publications, trade shows, and brown bag lunch sessions, where information can be shared from either internal or external sources.

INCENTIVE COMPENSATION

Another important element is having an incentive compensation plan. It depends on the nature of your business, but in many cases, this helps employees focus on performance targets and work hard to accomplish them. I designed many incentive plans during my career, and few of them worked out exactly as I hoped. From my experience, in spite of not being able to find the perfect formula, such a plan is still a motivating factor and should be one of the tools that might fit your organization and help you succeed. There are numerous elements that comprise incentive plans. At a minimum, participants should have a reasonable idea of the specific incentives they will receive if they and/or their team or department meet stated targets. Targets should be realistic; if not, the plan is apt to be counterproductive. Consider designating at least a portion of the reward payoff to overall enterprise targets (sales, profit, etc.). This will encourage teamwork. Part of the individual's or department's incentive targets should be directly related to that which they can mostly control. For example, the finance person or department may have little ability to control quality of customer service if that happens to be one of your plan targets. Communicate in advance that incentives will be paid only if 100 percent of the targets are met or that a stated percentage will be paid if less than 100 percent of the targets are achieved. The objective here is to connect your employees with the company's success through their own performance and success in accomplishing their jobs.

Some positions in a business, such as salespeople, are often compensated, at least in part, on an incentive basis tied to the sales they achieve. If your business requires non-sales staff to significantly participate in landing sales, this type of compensation can create resentment in the non-sales staff and reduce sales results, unless it's a minor element of the sales staff's compensation and/or the non-sales staff are also awarded incentive pay.

EMPLOYEE OWNERSHIP AND PROFIT SHARING

Eventual employee ownership is a benefit I strongly encourage you to consider (presuming it is appropriate for your kind of business), if not at this point in your startup phase, later on to help you grow your business. This may not be 100 percent true in all cases, but there is probable cause to believe, and my experience suggests, that employees who own a piece of the company they work for are more productive, have higher morale, are much less likely to leave, and better weigh the risks they take with the rewards that may come.

Most entrepreneurs find they are also the "Chief Worriers." When they have key employees who also have ownership, they tend to automatically also take a share of the "worrying" part. Unfortunately, there's only 100 percent of the ownership pie. Considering whether to share ownership is a serious decision and one that is not easily reversed. It can, however, be a powerful tool in recruiting and keeping key people.

As an example, in my case, it was one of the fundamental tools that I used in building a global business. I mentioned earlier that I founded my business in 1977 with aspirations of a national consulting practice in 10 years. A key element in making that happen was recognizing that although we are one country, there are distinct differences between geographical regions. From prior experience, I envisioned establishing 10 regional companies that collectively covered the continental 48 states. The first step was to find key partners in each of these 10 regions. In each case, I looked for one or more individuals whom I thought had the capacity to successfully build a regional business as part of a national whole. These individuals needed to be sellers/doers with the education and experience to develop new clients and the applicable technical skills and knowledge of environmental pollution issues to personally fulfill client needs. Preferably these future partners and entrepreneurs already resided in this region and spent a good part of their working career there, with familiarity with government regulations in their area and local business practices, as well as connections with potential clients and employees. They needed to buy into and adopt our culture, value system, and business philosophy. They also needed some business skills.

These people by definition were difficult to find. In my case, I identified a number of the affiliate entrepreneurs from my previous employment experience. In some cases, I found them through professional contacts of mine who knew them. In one case, I acquired half of an existing regional business. The ownership in each of these affiliated companies was 50 percent owned by my original partners, with the new regional partner owning the other 50 percent. In a couple cases, the second 50 percent was divided among several individuals in the initial regional team. In all cases, it was understood that the original regional partners would commit to finding additional partners in the future, who in turn could help build the business. In those cases, holding company partners (myself and my original partners) would sell share per share with the original regional partner or partners in the affiliate organization until we reached a minimum of one-third equity interest. After that, the affiliate partners could sell additional shares held by them to additional future partners in that affiliate if they wished.

In another case, when my company acquired a small UK consulting practice, Environmental Resources, Ltd., I wanted to ensure, as best I could, that the senior staff stayed. Toward that end, we gave them—at no cost—one-sixth of the equity post-acquisition. Performance targets were mutually agreed upon, and if reached (and they were), the senior staff was given another one-sixth share—again without cost. This turned out to be a great investment for both parties.

There's more than one way to address the fact that there can only be 100 percent ownership in any one business. If you own 10 regional companies, now you have 10 times that, or 1,000 percent, to utilize in attracting and keeping hard-to-find employees to help build the business. This strategy worked well. As I stated earlier, we successfully established 11 regional businesses in nine calendar years. In that time, the company's sales grew from zero to $35 million. In the next 15 years, with the addition of new international affiliates and specialized companies, we grew to 66 companies in 34 countries with about $320 million in revenue.

Each of the grassroots startups were capitalized with our holding company contributing half of the startup capital, and the other half came from affiliate partner(s). In some cases, affiliate partners made their contribution by agreeing to work for a set amount of time without compensation or at a much lower salary than they were entitled.

This structure wasn't the only component that led to the success of our business. Others were our vision and strategy, being in the right place at the right time, and our culture, which attracted and kept high-performing, talented staff.

Shadow or phantom stock is one vehicle to give employees the feeling of ownership without actually having it. For instance, employees are given certificates and contractual documents that look and feel like equity, but legally aren't. Phantom stock can be designed to shadow the company's real stock as it changes in value. I could write a whole chapter just on this subject exploring the nuances of various forms of incentive compensation that look like ownership. Employees have no legal liability; distributions they may receive that are tied to company's earnings or actual stock value are treated as ordinary income, similar to the ultimate gain they may experience when they redeem their phantom stock.

To gain some of the benefits of granting ownership to employees without actually doing so, you could implement a profit-sharing plan. You can set up such a plan on an annual basis, or you can average the benefits over longer periods of time and condition them on continuing employment. This approach can be fine-tuned, similar to the phantom stock, to specific circumstances in your particular business. I encourage you to conduct your own research and explore further as much has been written and published on this subject.

The more you can align employee interests with your own, the more likely you are to foster a successful business. When incorporated well into your business model and operations, these plans become good investments as they tend to attract the best talent and a motivated and highly productive workforce. Personally speaking, my partners and I enjoyed seeing employees do well. They were the main reason our business was also doing well. Naturally, employees also took some risk relative to their total compensation if the company experienced a down year.

Most of the ideas shared in this particular chapter are more relevant to some businesses than others. Every successful entrepreneur needs some familiarity with competitors' policies. Some human resources practices are so common among your competitors that there becomes a necessity to match them, as much as possible, from day one. Other benefits can separate you from the pack. It is not my intent to suggest all of these should be implemented from the beginning. You need to pick and choose those ideas that make the most sense for your particular business right now, while creating room to add others as your business grows.

GIVING BACK TO OTHERS

This subject is likely not at the top of your mind as you just start your business or identify ways to kick it into a higher gear, but for many businesses, employees, to some extent, will be a part of the "millennial" generation. This generation and the ones that follow are much more attuned to giving back to the community than previous generations. Companies that encourage their employees to be active in their community, in some capacity, are companies, all elements being equal, for which employees *want* to work. It's been my personal experience that employees want to work for a company that thinks about others outside the business in addition to growing their bottom line. I encourage you to consider making this part of your culture.

A company itself can donate to community nonprofit organizations, coach little league teams, participate in Scouting, or support local food banks, YMCA, Toys for Tots, etc. Often these efforts do not involve significant amounts of money, but they give the company visibility and make employees feel like they work for a company that cares and contributes to the community. It's important to draw the distinction between encouraging and pressuring employees. Companies that use high-pressure tactics usually find these altruistic efforts backfire; employees need to feel it's their choice.

One of the more rewarding examples of giving back to the community, which meant a great deal to many of the employees of a company for which I served on the board for the past 20 years, was to adopt a grade school. The students came from an underserved portion of our metropolitan area. The company established this relationship many years ago, and employees are given the opportunity (note: it is not required) to assist teachers with students who need extra help. One day a year, students are bussed (at the company's expense) to the business offices, where they are divided up and assigned to an individual employee to shadow them for the day. The company provides lunch and an opportunity for the students at the end of the day to share what they learned. This is just one example of a creative way for a business at a relatively small cost to make a difference in their community by providing their employees with an opportunity to personally make a difference. Most communities have all kinds of similar opportunities, whether in support of the police (PAL) organization, a YMCA, boys'/girls' clubs, senior centers, local food cupboard, etc.

There are other ways that the company can show that it cares for the community without incurring significant costs. You, as the owner, or one of your partners or employees can join and participate in a service club in your community such as Rotary, Lions, or Kiwanis. This also increases your company's visibility to the businesspeople in your community. In some cases, these contacts can also benefit your business.

Another low-cost and often employee-valued practice is to encourage employees to participate in community food drives and provide assistance to others when tragedy strikes. Giving employees the message that you value their participation in the community by coaching or refereeing little league or volunteering at the community hospital can create very positive feelings of pride for the company. Giving time off to volunteer in the local school as an occasional teaching assistant, at the volunteer fire company, or with disadvantaged young people are some of the numerous ways to create a community-enrichment program.

In my case, I sensed our employees were looking for an opportunity to apply their professional skills to improving our natural environment outside their regular work assignments. I encouraged one of my partners with previous experience in this area to incorporate a 501(c)(3) foundation. The ERM Foundation was legally independent from the company and focused on working with nonprofits that wanted to improve sanitation, water supply, environmental education, or impacts from climate change. This aligned with an environmental consulting firm. The trustees of the foundation were elected from among our employees.

The ERM Foundation set up a website, soliciting applications from nonprofit organizations throughout the world. A volunteer committee then screened applications and made recommendations for funding.

Another committee raised funds each year. The campaign was conducted among our employees worldwide. Some chose to raise funds externally through bake sales, bike races, or other creative, fun ways. In most cases, though, people decided to contribute either in cash or through payroll deduction. Again, I want to emphasize the voluntary nature of the endeavor for employees to participate and to what extent. Their participation or lack thereof had no effect on their career, promotions, etc. The company matched 50 percent to dollar-for-dollar the funds that the employees raised.

Individuals also contributed their professional expertise on a pro bono basis. The company evaluated these requests on a case-by-case basis, and in some instances, this work added to the employee's experience, which was later valuable in commercial paid assignments.

Since the ERM Foundation's founding in 1994 through 2020, it has awarded $4.5 million to support 609 projects with 209 different organizations in 47 counties. In an average year, 400 employees donated, and 300 volunteered in some capacity. All of this activity stemmed from only the U.S.-based employees. The company also set up ERM Foundations in the UK, Germany, and Australia. Even though I retired from the business some 20 years ago, the foundation continues to be highly valued by the company's employees. I mention this not necessarily as practical for a startup business but to plant a seed that, should your organization succeed and grow, there may be a point in the future when you could exercise your entrepreneurial skills while giving back to a world that badly needs the help.

Staffing your business with the "right" people makes it a lot easier to accomplish your goals. You also need sales. How do you build your brand and bring on the buyers you need to make your business succeed? See the next chapter for ideas on this topic.

— CHAPTER 6 —

MARKETING AND SALES

There's a saying: "Love makes the world go around." The business equivalent is "Sales makes the business go around." Without sales, nothing else matters. This chapter will address marketing, sales, and the care and nurturing of customers.

Marketing, as I use the term, is about gaining awareness of your brand and products/services and identifying and successfully selling to potential customers. It is the means of attracting, keeping, and influencing customers to conduct business with you.

When you start a business from scratch, you typically have to account for all of these elements on a shoestring budget, for better or worse, or by yourself. However, there are others available on a hire-for-the-task basis who can help.

Your marketing strategy will flow directly from your business strategy. Your "unique selling proposition" weighs your competitive advantages versus competitors, such as price, service, quality, unique technology, convenience, etc.

An important part of this strategy is to focus on customer market segments where you demonstrate a competitive advantage. A great mistake that many startups and some more mature businesses make is trying to be all things to all people (or too many things to too many people). With limited resources, you have to focus on the customers and products/services that most align for your best chances of success. Forget the long shots, no matter how attractive. You can't afford them.

FINDING CUSTOMERS

Each type of business has its own unique challenges: to identify, contact, and influence potential customers. For example, if you start a retail florist business, the customer base you want includes wedding planners, funeral directors, local churches, synagogues, and other local businesses likely to buy fresh flowers, in addition to the general community. Likewise, if you start a trucking and transportation business, you need to identify an entirely different group of prospects. Regardless of your business niche, potential customer information should be acquired, much of which is available in the public domain for no cost. The other secret is knowing where to look. This is a case where some one-time outside help in the beginning may pay big dividends finding the customers you want much sooner than you could otherwise on your own. Your local reference librarian, who can help you locate online resources, is a good place to start. If your customers are other businesses, what titles do likely buyers have in these businesses? What size are these businesses?

If you want to market to certain types of businesses, identify them using their standard industrial classification (SIC) code, which is found in a database the federal government maintains.

Some entrepreneurs work with a wide variety of businesses with great success by scaling their business using an online technique called "quiz funnels," which attract prospects and convert them to buyers. One of the marketing thought leaders in this area is Ryan Levesque. You may want to check out his website, The ASK Method Co. (https://askmethod.com), or his book.[8]

Certain firms can also provide you with sales leads for your business. The tools they typically use entail white papers on a subject relevant to your business and hopefully valuable to the recipient. These can be sent via email to recipients targeted based on their business size, location, the prospective buyer's title, etc. It can be surprisingly inexpensive. It may cost you $50 to $100 for a lead, for example. Ryan Levesque's quiz funnel concept claims to produce leads below a dollar each.

Never overlook partners or employees with experience in the market you want to enter or contacts that can lead to potential sales opportunities.

Conferences and trade shows can be valuable places to find potential customers and leads. They are also excellent sources to size up your competition, gain exposure to purchasing agents and distributors, meet with potential buyers, and increase the visibility of your business. Which trade associations are closely aligned with your business? If you have not already joined them, consider doing so. Many associations use an affordable fee structure for small startup businesses. Check out their websites.

---

8 Ryan Levesque, *Ask: The Counterintuitive Online Method to Discover Exactly What Your Customers Want to Buy...Create a Mass of Raving Fans...and Take any Business to the Next Level* (Carlsbad: Hay House Business, 2019). Ryan Levesque, *Choose: The Single Most Important Decision Before Starting Your Business* (Carlsbad: Hay House Business, 2019)

PROMOTION

Three areas of promotion are important to most businesses: paid media (advertising), unpaid media (public relations), and sales promotion materials. Common to advertising and sales promotion are your business name, graphics, and colors used for your business name/logo on all key promotion materials like brochures, business cards, stationery, catalogs, and flyers. Consistent branding is an important marketing component with long-term implications that will greatly benefit from professional assistance. This is not usually a budget-busting expense, and many small or single-person advertising and/or graphic design firms exist almost everywhere. You can find them on the Internet or by referral from people you know. They will happily supply samples of their previous work for other clients.

ADVERTISING

We are all familiar with advertising—bombarded with it day in and day out. At the turn of the last century, a major retailer that spent vast amounts on advertising said, "I know at least half of what I spend on advertising is wasted; I just don't know which half."[9] We all know of advertising in newspapers, billboards, trade publications, general interest magazines, T.V., the Internet, signage at ballparks, musical venues, etc. Now, high-tech digital billboards can carry more sophisticated messaging. We also have much higher targeting in terms of digital media. It's not a coincidence when you inquire about auto insurance via the

9 Source: John Wanamaker

Internet and then suddenly you're seeing ads from other insurance companies popping up on your digital devices.

As a general rule, the more business you aim at consumers, the more advertising, in one form or another, should comprise part of your marketing plan. **Pay attention to your competitors** as one reference point. Advertising is a powerful tool when used in a creative and targeted fashion.

If advertising is part of your communications mix, you will need professional help. Advertising agencies come in many shapes, sizes, and costs. You definitely want to work with one with relevant experience to your business. Most agencies/services will not work for direct competitors at the same time, but some may have worked in your industry or a closely related one in the past. Seek advice from people you know who use advertising agencies, the Internet, or a local ad club.

PUBLIC RELATIONS

Public relations firms can be very helpful in building your image and brand and increasing customer awareness. These professionals specialize in increasing your company's profile in magazines, social media, newspapers, and broadcast media (both printed and electronic). They also place articles of interest to your current and potential customers. Like every other service, they come in all sizes, qualities, and costs. As mentioned previously, during your startup phase, utilizing freelancers is very cost-effective. As your business grows, it may be worthwhile to entertain a more full-service firm, as opposed to building that capability internally. One of the other considerations, should you want to explore this at some point, is to check with your trade associations and competitors to help identify firms that understand your particular business niche. Firms that generally represent manufacturers won't do as good a job, for example, if you are in the logistics business, as one that focuses on your particular niche. This can sometimes be a problem as some firms may have the expertise you want, but they are forbidden by their clients from working with competitors. It's important to find an outside firm that will appreciate you as a client. It's probably not the best place for you to be a minnow if your outside supplier is already serving whales. Even a firm that specializes in your arena still requires time to learn how you operate, so consider the likelihood of longevity with the team assigned to you. Their turnover can be expensive for you. In some cases, businesses gain visibility and credibility by publishing articles of interest to potential buyers in trade or professional publications. Making the most of this route requires time, connections, and content, but the exposure is often worth it.

A public relations resource can also help you build a library of white papers demonstrating your professional or business insights and skills. These are most commonly distributed electronically today (and kept in a library on your website), but an attractive, occasional paper mailing to key customers and prospects can provide impressions of the firm's quality and professionalism. Just ensure mailings have value for your intended audience.

If you specialize in a broad-based industry, you can buy prospect lists. However, the response rate on these kinds of unsolicited mailings is very low, and there are legal restrictions on unsolicited emails in some cases—less so for postal mailing.

The goal is to make every customer a repeat customer. For instance, if you own a beer distributor store, besides convenience and price, building a loyal customer base could mean keeping them informed about new brews, breweries, local events, etc.

SOCIAL MEDIA

In my experience, social media is particularly effective for consumer-type businesses, though less so for business-to-business transactions. You will need to evaluate whether social media marketing has applicability for your particular business. Social media sites are very helpful in promoting your business and attracting potential employees.

Hiring outside help to manage these types of promotions can be affordable even for startups. Many freelancers now provide social media services, and even small public relations firms offer these services now as well. As smaller players themselves, they will give you the attention that is often harder to receive from those set up to serve much larger clients.

SALES PROMOTION MATERIALS

Sales promotion materials are inexpensive but very important tools to communicate the quality of your organization's products and professionalism. Printed materials, such as brochures, business cards, and sales flyers, should share a consistent design, which you can easily achieve through a freelance designer or small graphics firm. The same design elements should also appear in electronic communications: emails, newsletters, proposals, and other sales literature, and even your website banner.

Some entrepreneurs are switching to hybrid or virtual business cards. These can be physical cards with QR codes, scannable digital cards, or chips embedded in physical objects. The latter allows the contact information to transfer by tapping the object. These high-tech options make it easier for potential customers to file and store your information electronically. It also may make it a more memorable experience for those you meet.

YOUR WEBSITE

In today's world, your website is a crucial communication tool. It provides key information about the company: products/services, locations, company philosophy and history, and customer testimonials. Many small design firms and freelance designers also provide website design services (just Google web design for your city). It helps any designer you hire to show them existing websites with elements that you admire and would like included on your site.

CIVIC ORGANIZATIONS

Another route that many found useful is to join civic organizations, such as the local chamber of commerce or industrial development council—they are known by various names in different locales. As mentioned earlier, I urge you to check out local service clubs, such as the Rotary, Lions, or, depending on your age, the Junior Chamber of Commerce. These kinds of organizations can provide you with visibility in your community and access to potential customers or suppliers.

BUSINESS ROUNDTABLE

Business roundtables are an idea less likely to apply in a startup scenario but could serve as a powerful tool for established businesses and, down the road, for new entrepreneurs. One of my partners established a business roundtable (think customers) made up of senior executives from our client group, such as vice presidents with responsibility for their company's environmental affairs. Once a year, we hosted a two-day meeting, by invitation only, at a popular resort. My company facilitated the meeting and developed an agenda centered around subjects of interest in that particular year. The members found this valuable for several reasons. Among them was that they had no other platform in which to exchange ideas with people with similar responsibilities outside of their industry. For example, a textile manufacturer could share experiences with someone in a steel or oil refining business. Some of the presentations were made by our staff and some by attendees. We did not attempt to use this as a selling opportunity; we benefited from our clients selling each other on our capabilities. As often happened, the professional services we provided one client attendee were passed along to another attendee with an implied recommendation. This proved to be a very effective marketing tool.

In addition to strengthening our relationships with clients, this event also provided a vehicle to learn more about our clients' concerns and keep us attuned to their future needs. Our company bore the cost for the venue, meals, lodging (excluding one's family members), and materials, and each attendee was responsible for their own travel. We interspersed the meeting with opportunities for golf, tennis, relaxation, or downtime. The meeting was so popular that administrative assistants often contacted us shortly after the meeting to obtain the date for the next year's gathering to block off on their boss's calendars.

HOSTING AND SPONSORING EVENTS

At the right time and place, whether at trade shows or conferences, hosting is an effective way of thanking existing customers and meeting new ones. ERM, for many years, hosted clients at an annual conference that many routinely attended. The conference was held in various places around the United States, usually localities that present special entertainment or experiences. We typically invited clients several months in advance of this conference, which was always held in the fall. The formal invitation included the details of the sponsored event. One of the more memorable ones happened in San Francisco in 1989, the year of the last great earthquake. In this instance, we chartered a fairly large yacht and planned to provide our guests with cocktails and dinner along with a cruise around Alcatraz Island, home of San Quentin State Prison. The earthquake struck at the time when most people were getting ready and/or making their way to the waterfront and our chartered yacht. Almost all of our guests managed to board the vessel despite lacking electric power and functioning traffic lights. Because of the earthquake, transportation and communications in the bay area were severely disrupted. Eventually, government authorities commandeered our yacht to use as temporary transportation to transport people back and forth between San Francisco and Oakland, as the Oakland Bay Bridge had partially collapsed.

Resisting this "suggestion" was fruitless and certainly not in the public interest. I asked the person in authority if they planned to take another large yacht berthed next to us. They said, "No." I then asked if they would assist me explaining their good fortune and asking if they minded making room for our guests. Luckily, they acquiesced. In the meantime, we watched local events on the television in the new yacht, operating on its own independent power supply, from the vantage point of the blimp hovering over Candlestick Park Stadium. Fun fact: the stadium hosted a World Series baseball game that night. Following that event, we sent each of our guests t-shirts that read, *I Survived the 1989 San Francisco Earthquake*. Needless to say, years later, we heard feedback from those in attendance that they would never forget that event. This may not be an appropriate tool to use in the first few years in business, but you never know what might become a vehicle that helps expand your business.

OPEN HOUSE

Consider hosting an open house after your initial efforts are in place to start your business. It is customary to include your employees and their families, your accountants, outside advisors such as your lender and attorney, your suppliers, and certainly any existing customers. If you can attract prospective customers, that's even better. An open house doesn't need to be expensive to be effective.

REFERRALS

Promotional potential also lies in others who might influence customers your way. In my case, environmental attorneys were people I wanted to know. We made an effort to identify the leading environmental attorneys to make them aware of our capabilities. To some extent, the attorneys also viewed us as possible connections for future potential clients. Whom might those interested parties be in your case?

CUSTOMER TESTIMONIALS

Most businesses encourage customer testimonials for use in sales literature and on their websites. Most of us are influenced by previous customer ratings and recommendations. The best time to request these is after completing an assignment, contract, or sale, especially if you know the customer is particularly pleased. This kind of material, if pre-approved, can be used in the variety of your marketing materials and sales literature. Sometimes customers are willing to take inquiries from prospective customers, which also yields positive feedback and valuable leads.

SELLING

Selling can include a few sales of very large ticket items a year or many items a day in a retail operation. Businesses at both ends of the spectrum work hard to build their brands, create demand for their products or services, and engage with customers to the point where they are ready to buy. They all work to earn repeat customers, which means satisfied customers. They need to be satisfied with the quality, service, and treatment. The customer needs to feel the value to return.

Sales pay the bills. Successful businesses really make an effort to ensure that all employees accept that they are part of the sales effort, whether they work in accounting or a warehouse. They see their job as part of making sure the sale happens and the customer is satisfied. It's a mindset that should be encouraged.

Many professional or technical service organizations are populated with staff who don't consider themselves salespeople; they don't like to sell, don't think they can, or, worse yet, they think it's beneath them.

This can be true in other business types, too. Their attitudes are counterproductive to the growth of the business. The good news is their attitudes can be changed. There are training programs that can aid in making this transition in people's minds.

Decades ago, I discovered, through an American Management Association seminar, an individual named Maynard Garfield. His small company put together a sales training program called Persuasive Communications. While Maynard has since passed, his organization still exists. We used his training program for many years to build a common sales language among the professionals throughout our organization. There are others like him who also can help.

In my case, we used the seller-doer approach. Senior professionals responsible for projects in their area of expertise had the primary role in developing business. Clients liked the idea that they talked to people who technically understood their problems and the alternatives available to solve them. They liked the idea that the person who "sold them" was also the person responsible to "deliver" the final product. This methodology doesn't work for all types of businesses, but it does for many. It also can be more cost-effective than other ways of selling.

Depending on your type of business, you might want to consider one of the following as an alternative or in addition to employing your own sales force. For the startup company, the cost of making a sale is crucial. Some use sales representatives. In some cases, these sales representatives are exclusive in representing only you; in other cases, they may represent other complementary, but seldom competing, lines of services or products. In our digital age, some businesses automate sales as customers buy their products online. Some businesses develop sales by paying for referrals to those who may touch your customer. For instance, if you are in the home painting business, you may set up referrals with other craftsmen who work for customers who need your services. Sometimes, this occurs where no money exchanges hands; it's simply a matter of mutual support.

The nature of your business may benefit from teaming with others on an occasional one-off or a routine basis to satisfy customers looking for more than what your organization can supply by itself.

GOVERNMENT SALES

If your business focuses, at least partially, on selling to one level of government or another, selling mechanisms may be different in some respects. Whether selling to private or government parties, customer relationships make a difference. Customers like to conduct business with people they know, can relate to, and respect. If your company typically deals with purchasing agents in the public or private sector, you need to tackle the challenging task of getting to know the individuals at those organizations. Typically, they want a list of your qualifications, experience, previous projects, services, or products relevant or apropos to their needs, along with any previous business conducted at specific government, or related entity, locations, or branches. Wining and dining may be a customary expectation; it's a bit of an art form to figure out how appropriate it is. Some organizations and most governmental agencies forbid employees from accepting "gifts" of more than trivial value from a potential vendor—it can be the kiss of death if you participate in these types of practices.

The federal government, states, and some local governments routinely publish or post requests for bids on supplies and services they wish to purchase. This information is available for free on the Internet.

Your product or service price is almost always a consideration. The degree to which it influences a sale varies greatly, depending on that product or service, the competitive environment, and the buyer. Price is usually more important in situations where buyers use a competitive bid purchasing process and have the perception (often incorrectly) that the product or service is essentially the same regardless of the supplier. Government staff are loath to endure criticism when they select anyone other than the lowest bidder. They must justify their rationale. My experience is that the private-sector buyer is often more concerned with ultimate value, quality, long-term life-cycle costs, customer service after the sale, and the strength of the supplier.

It is fairly common, when contracting with the federal government and sometimes with local government (but rare in the private sector), to subject the supplier to a post-purchase audit with claw-back (recovery) rights. The government employs such contracts when they pay for products or services on the basis of direct cost plus overhead with a stated profit margin. Your business should have a software accounting system to track all costs using standard accounting principles. This necessary information allows you to know your exact direct costs and overhead items, as well as profitability on any given contract. The problem, if there is one, tends to occur in classifying allowable overhead expenses. Government agencies, not uncommonly, disallow costs that you—hopefully in good faith—include in your overhead. I personally know a couple of instances in which firms knowingly included nonallowable items and/or otherwise inflated costs, resulting in the government seeking civil damages and successfully pursuing senior executives with criminal prosecution.

SALES PROPOSALS

For some businesses, excluding retail, the selling process includes the preparation of proposals or quotes for the service or product that the buyer seeks. This is often done even for a sole-source purchase. The art of preparing winning proposals, which can be a time-consuming and expensive exercise, is an extensive subject in and of itself. However, it is important that the appearance of your sales proposal, including the layout and graphics, look "professional" and reflect positively on your company.

Most businesses learn to automate most of the process by assembling the standard elements in an appropriate way for particular customers. I caution you in preparing such automated messaging; you don't want to make it obvious that special attention was not paid. Most buyers want to feel worthy of a customized proposal.

In addition to describing exactly that which you plan to furnish, proposals contain the terms and conditions for the sale. My general advice is to write down the product or service you will provide in as much detail as necessary to minimize the chance of mutual misunderstanding of your intent and your customer's expectations. Those terms and conditions usually include the agreed-upon price, in an itemized list of components, as well as a delivery and payment timetable. They address insurance, liability, and authorized parties, among other factors. The proposal or quote may in fact be a contract if the other party accepts it. Needless to say, you need legal advice in developing your standard documents. If you deviate from these documents, I strongly encourage you to again obtain legal advice before you commit any further resources.

In some cases, your customer will insist on using their own standard contracts and terms. Again, in this instance, obtain legal advice regarding the terms that your company finds acceptable to the specifics of the situation.

One of the lessons I learned very early in my career relative to giving a prospective customer a dollar figure involves the question, "What do you think this will cost?" Unless this is an off-the-shelf item with a fixed price or you know the precise cost, it is unwise to give a direct answer. The reason is, invariably, that when estimating the work and cost in detail, it almost always yields a higher figure than you initially provided to your prospective customer. No matter how many caveats you add when giving an estimate, that figure is the one they will have in their minds. It's far better to say, "I will be able to give you that figure once I pull all the pieces together." Perhaps they will settle for a half-serious answer, such as, "Well, I know it's going to be more than a thousand and less than a million."

PRICING

There are a number of ways to price a product or service. In the United States, we are used to retail pricing and services based on a fixed price per item. Many international travelers know business is conducted differently elsewhere in some parts of the world. For many countries, this is just the starting point. The ultimate price is determined by a negotiation. As an aside, I found in some instances even in the States, the fixed price of an item can, on occasion, be negotiated. For instance, sometimes a merchant discounts an item if you pay with cash versus using credit, even though they don't advertise this option. On occasion, if you buy in quantity, even without indication of a discount, the seller gives one if requested. Other forms of pricing include a time and materials, or cost-plus, type of contract, which is often used particularly with an unknown scope of work. Again, in these instances, it's not uncommon to use a "cost-not-to-exceed"/"subject to change" if the buyer approves changes in scope. In my experience, where possible, avoid a time and materials or cost-plus contract with a guaranteed maximum. If the project or purchasing scope is fuzzy, it can lead to either a loss and/or an unhappy client, particularly with incremental scope creep that is often difficult to document.

An incentive contract may be appropriate. In an incentive contract, the ultimate price the buyer pays might depend on when the goods and services are ultimately delivered. As an example, the seller usually receives a premium for completing the work earlier than the target date or accrues a penalty if completing the work after that date. Sometimes an incentive contract is used when there are anticipated savings as a result of user improvements. The seller might receive a share of the savings for a specified time. Another instance is when the buyer pays less if they purchase other additional items within a certain timeframe.

Starting your own business entails taking on unique risks, beyond those for general employees. The next chapter will discuss some of the major risk categories and methods to mitigate them.

— CHAPTER 7 —

RECOGNIZING AND MANAGING MAJOR BUSINESS RISKS

The risk of unplanned, unwanted events is inherent in living. Businesses are almost by definition risky endeavors. Unanticipated events and circumstances are among the reasons many businesses fail. Some risks can and should be anticipated. If you can visualize the risk in advance, you have a better chance to mitigate it or avoid it all together. This chapter will feature some of the basic risks that apply to most businesses. This is by no means an exhaustive coverage of this subject, but it will inform or remind you to consider how to minimize them in your business. It also serves as a way that you, as a new entrepreneur, can check against your tolerance for risk. You increase the odds of succeeding by minimizing your exposure to each of these. As the old saying goes, being forewarned is being forearmed.

Before we move on, you should also note that the other side of risk is opportunity. One business's loss or risk of loss is another business's opportunity. That's why there are businesses that specialize in remediating the damage caused by floods, fires, mold, theft, IT defenses, etc.

LOSS OF KEY EMPLOYEES

Losing key employees is a risk for every business, but it's particularly challenging in instances where individuals leave who possess key skills on which the business depends. These cases impact the company's reputation and can be particularly damaging if that individual transfers to work for a competitor. Related high-risk areas are situations where the departing person has strong relationships with major accounts and is likely to take that account with them as they seek future employment. To mitigate this risk, it's always better to have redundant skill sets in critical job functions and multiple staff who establish relationships with key accounts. It won't necessarily eliminate the pain, but it will greatly reduce the impact. In some instances, this risk can be mitigated with a noncompete agreement that a qualified attorney can develop for you. However, such agreements are limited in time and distance, include consideration (of monetary value for the employee), and meet specific requirements under state law. Some states significantly hinder the enforcement of these agreements.

CUSTOMER DIVERSIFICATION

It's always better for any business to have a diversified portfolio of customers. For a business dependent on a few major accounts, it could be catastrophic if those accounts no longer conduct business with you, for any variety of reasons. For example, perhaps your relationship manager leaves your company and takes certain accounts with them. Personnel changes on the customer's end can sometimes, through no fault of your own, result in business transferring to a competitor. Also, consolidation of purchasing activity with new, unfamiliar decision-makers results in a loss of business. These are just a few reasons to, wherever possible, diversify your customer base. Ideally, you should diversify into different sectors of the economy and geographical regions to minimize the impact of the ups and downs of business activity. This type of risk will always be part of your business environment.

CUSTOMER CREDIT RISK

If your business isn't paid at the time the client or customer buys, there is a risk that they won't pay. Presale credit checks, partial or total prepayment terms, and proactive dispute resolution efforts are possible means of minimizing losses. Billing directly after the sale is also a way to minimize payment disputes, as well as to reduce working capital. If a significant amount of time passes, customers' memories can fail or change with respect to the agreement—your delivery of a product or service and their particular payment.

RISK OF LEVERAGE

Using borrowed money to grow a business is one of the elements at the heart of the free enterprise or capitalist system. Some business sectors in particular are major users of debt, such as real estate and property development. However, too much debt can be disastrous. If earnings falter, asset values drop significantly, and/or interest rates rise, repayment may not be feasible. Consider these factors when you need or use financing.

Note that most lending institutions require you to pledge assets as security for funds they lend. This could entail marketable securities as well as your business or real property. For many startups, this means a personal (joint, if married) guarantee and perhaps a second or third mortgage on your personal residence.

LOSS OF CREDIT

Most businesses rely on credit from a lending institution to fulfill the working capital needed to acquire equipment, finance inventory, etc. Lenders are eager to lend well-capitalized businesses that could—if they wanted to—operate without borrowing, and they are usually very reluctant to lend when the business desperately needs the funds. It pays to establish a solid relationship with your lender. Your credibility is directly related to your credit capacity. You establish credibility by always openly sharing bad, as well as good, news in a timely manner. Meeting your projections a high percentage of the time builds confidence that you will do so in the future, too, where your lender is counting on that to repay your loan.

A personal example might be instructive. In addition to my primary business, I was an active partner in a number of other businesses that developed, owned, and operated continuing care retirement communities (CCRCs) in several states; a marina; adjoining waterfront homes with a boathouse; and rental homes. All of these businesses utilized substantial debt. During the Great Recession in 2007-2009, the real estate market took a nosedive, and senior citizens couldn't find buyers for their homes to move into a CCRC. Unemployment also skyrocketed, which significantly reduced leisure expenditures and hammered the second-home market. Although these businesses were located in different parts of the country and different business sectors, they all were devastated by the depth and breadth of the recession. The result was workouts with multiple banks over multiple years. Not a great experience, I can assure you.

ECONOMIC CYCLES

Very few businesses are immune from recessions and other local, natural, or global elements. For instance, we just recently endured a global pandemic that negatively affected millions of businesses worldwide. Some related risks include recessions that never affect every area of the economy equally, weather events, power and utility outages such as those experienced in Texas in 2020, government regulations and/or legislation that can increase or decrease your market overnight, and technology that is both a blessing and a curse in terms of its impact on your business. I'm sure you can think of others, but some of these risks can be mitigated through insurance, at a cost. Others are just the kind that may keep you awake at night.

REGULATORY COMPLIANCE

Regulatory compliance is an arena in which ignorance is not bliss. Business startups can seldom afford specialists in all aspects of the law or regulations with which you are expected to comply. Sometimes entrepreneurs find themselves in trouble innocently, while others, on occasion, knowingly skirt the law. The law in this area is so extensive as to make complete compilation here impossible, but in general, most of us are aware of legal requirements with respect to hiring, firing, and compensating people. Compliance with occupational, safety, and health (OSHA) and environmental regulations are concerns for some types of businesses, as well as advertising, product safety, etc. This gives you some flavor of areas that entrepreneurs should educate themselves on and, where possible, rely on outside expertise to minimize the chances that they innocently operate outside of the law; repercussions can be serious indeed. Sometimes the regulations address relatively innocuous items, such as signage for your business, and other times, they pertain to items of a more serious magnitude, such as operating permits, collection and disbursement of the government authority's sales taxes, Social Security and income tax withholding. and remittance and record keeping.

OBSOLESCENCE

When I think about risk of obsolescence, I think of those that affect us inside our businesses as well as those that are imposed upon us by outside forces. A business can become less competitive and therefore more at risk of failure by not adapting in time to more efficient or effective ways of conducting business. A "we've always done it this way" mindset could put a business in jeopardy. Obsolescence can occur in equipment, systems, and employees who can't or won't adapt or develop new skills. It can make it more difficult to keep younger, "hip" employees or hire new staff. This category of risk is seldom a threat to a business in the beginning, as it takes time to grow moss on people, methods, and equipment. Normally, the external threats of obsolescence are not an issue in the beginning either, but they can become major threats as a business matures. As tastes change, needs arise, old ones disappear, and competitors appear on the scene with a better mousetrap.

Recent examples of rigidity or inability to see future trends and adapt include the Eastman Kodak film business and digital photography, the Blackberry and the iPhone, IBM wedded to its mainframe computers versus personal computers, and Steve Jobs's resistance in deviating from the Apple computer to take on the iPhone.

As we all know, life, and certainly technology, is changing at an accelerating pace, and in some cases, it doesn't take as long as it used to before you find yourself facing obsolescence. An area affecting many businesses today, which will affect almost everyone eventually, is the adoption of artificial intelligence and robotics as they become more capable of performing many functions, including high-level tasks we once thought only people could perform. A point to consider as you launch a business is *how do you take advantage of this technology?* The highlights of McKinsey & Company, an economics research and management consulting firm, covering 54 countries analyzing the effects of automation on the global labor market, "Automation Invasion," can be found in Appendix 3.[10] Their assessment indicates substantial impacts in almost all economic sectors and across the globe by 2030. For instance, their report indicates 237 million manufacturing employees or 34 percent worldwide will be replaced by automation. Similar results are predicted for construction with a loss of 82 million jobs or 54 percent of those currently employed. In the transportation and warehousing sector, it's 41 million—34 percent. They also reported the impact of

---

10 Kurt Snibbe, "Automation Invasion," Daily Local News, February 22, 2020, page A8.

automation on employment by country. They project 46 percent of jobs in the United States will be accomplished by automation by 2030. *Think about that!* How can you make this accelerating trend be a positive for your business?

REPUTATION

In some respects, businesses are like individuals. It takes most of us a long time to build a good reputation. That reputation can be ruined overnight with just one incident. It's true with businesses. A good reputation makes a difference. Most of us avoid people with a bad reputation where we can; the same is true with respect to those with which we choose to conduct business. Establishing a great reputation for your business starts and ends with you. It's up to you to see that the standards you set are adhered to by your employees. One bad apple, or a few bad apples, can cause a lot of damage to a business's reputation.

THEFT

Besides theft from outside your business, which we are naturally "wired" to protect ourselves from, there is also the risk of employee theft. Sometimes, a gambling or drug addiction issue causes an otherwise honest individual to steal. Sometimes, the circumstances in their home life raise the risk. It is possible to buy insurance to reduce the impact of such occurrences.

In my experience, the greatest area of exposure for theft is from employees with access to the company's checkbook. In my case, a bookkeeper/office support employee used company credit cards to purchase gift cards and postage and then resold them. She also falsified invoices and wrote checks that ultimately deposited into her personal account, resulting in a total loss of around $130,000. In another instance, a regional manager and authorized signatory generated invoices that were paid by the regional accountant.

This risk is particularly high in small businesses that can ill afford the loss. Small businesses also are prone to minimal checks and balances built into their systems, which minimizes the likelihood of this happening in the first place. To add insult to injury, in many cases, local prosecutors are often reluctant to expend scarce resources prosecuting employees who perpetrate white-collar crime.

There is also a risk of employees, or their outside accomplices, stealing raw materials, products, or services. These can be very difficult to detect. It is one of the reasons fast food drive-throughs have the customer pay at one window and receive their order at another. As another example, I recall a story of a West German who was employed in East Germany—when the country was divided—who passed through the East German checkpoint every afternoon after work, on foot, pushing a wheelbarrow with his lunch pail and tools. Each time, the guard, who suspected him of stealing, checked his wheelbarrow. Each time, he found nothing. After the reunification of Germany, the former guard enjoyed a beer at a local beer hall and spotted the workman he had stopped so many times. Confronting the man, whom he still suspected of theft, he asked what he stole and how he did it. Yes, he admitted, he stole wheelbarrows.

CYBERSECURITY

In recent years, a new form of theft emerged—hacking your business's IT system and demanding payment to return company access to your own files. Fortunately, the perpetrators of this type of crime are not apt to target a startup business. However, when you set up your IT systems, build in as much protection as possible, which likely requires outside expertise. It will pay dividends as you grow and your risk of becoming a target increases.

In a recent ad in the *Wall Street Journal*,[11] one specialty company that helps protect businesses from this risk said organizations spend $160 billion a year. In spite of this figure, a ransomware attack occurs every 11 seconds, and each year, it gets worse. Take heed!

LEGISLATION AND EXECUTIVE EDICTS

All businesses are expected to operate within the law. Some businesses exist *because* of the law, for example, in many states, if you want to sell substances such as alcoholic beverages. Legislation can, *overnight*, change which products can be sold and to whom and affect labor and material costs, among other factors. Some businesses rely on minimum wage labor. In many areas, societal forces are at work to significantly increase minimum hourly wages, which puts pressure on employers to raise prices, become more efficient, automate, or make other adjustments to accommodate the change in wages.

During times of natural disasters, wars, or a public-health crisis—such as the recent COVID-19 pandemic—government officials forced

---

11 Tanium, Inc. full page advertisement in The Wall Street Journal, July 14, 2022, page A5.

major changes that affected most of the economy. These forced closures—while probably necessary to protect public health and contain the threat—caused many thousands of businesses in the United States to close their doors for good. To make matters worse, many business disruption insurance policies excluded coverage for loss of business due to government action.

CLIMATE CHANGE, WEATHER, AND SUSTAINABILITY

Many recognize that climate change is happening at an accelerated pace. This presents opportunities for entrepreneurs to help businesses and individuals take action to mitigate the damages as well as their contribution to this phenomenon. This reality also presents a threat to some sectors of the economy. It also obviously affects weather patterns and, in turn, increases costs to combat potential damage from storms, forest fires, power outages, etc.

Again, as part of the bigger picture, your business will likely feel the impact of the post-World War II accelerated increase in global population, rising living standards, improved healthcare, and lengthening human lifespans. This resulted in huge increases in energy demand—largely met by fossil fuels—economies built on consumerism, and proliferating use of plastics, pesticides, and a host of other chemicals (many of which have unintended harmful effects to life and the critical natural systems). All of this puts pressure on life, land, water, and our atmosphere. The way most of us live in advanced economies, and the rest of the world trying to catch up, isn't sustainable without triggering changes in global climate that will have far-reaching effects on life and economies. We are depleting nonrenewable resources that will present huge challenges to find alternatives.

Why, you might ask, did I include this material? How does it relate to building a successful business? Recognition of this growing crisis presents many opportunities for new, and existing, businesses to provide services and products that will produce more with less, recover and reuse, harness renewable forms of energy, etc. Sooner or later, most, if not all, businesses will feel the pressure from public opinion, laws, regulations, economic factors, and competition to conduct their activities as sustainably as possible.

LITIGATION

Americans live in a society where lawsuits are very common. The list is long for exposure to potential lawsuits from public or private parties, as well as current or former employees. They can relate to your products or services, personnel practices, intellectual property rights, contracts for materials or services, etc.

Many of the documents customarily used by businesses, such as employment agreements, purchase orders, proposals/bids, contracts for services, materials, or products, human resources policies, leases, and loan documents, should be reviewed by competent legal counsel. When done correctly, these documents minimize litigation and losses, if litigation occurs.

Another effective way to ward off litigation is to bend over backward, if necessary, to rectify the situation or appease the other party. This is usually far cheaper—in dollars, time, and distraction—than litigation. In litigation, often the only winners are the attorneys. Sometimes, we humans feel that on *principle* we must engage in litigation. Often, though, such action comes at a much greater cost than fixing or settling. Lawsuits can take on a life of their own. Whatever time and money you think you will spend is probably much less than it will actually take. Our U.S. legal system is not known for efficiency or timeliness. Furthermore, there is no guarantee that justice will actually be achieved.

Good legal advice can also minimize losses by inserting liability limits and, where allowed and if appropriate, requiring arbitrators to settle disputes.

INSURANCE

Everyone is familiar with insurance—for your home, car, or life. Sometimes, we acquire insurance voluntarily to mitigate our own risk, or we are required to take it on to mitigate others' risk, such as mortgage insurance, which is designed to primarily protect the lender. Some of the risks discussed in this chapter can be mitigated by insurance. However, as we all know, by purchasing insurance, you take on a known and presumably manageable expense in exchange for minimizing risk (the probability of which may be very small) of a catastrophic loss, such as insurance coverage for casualty losses from fire, water, or wind.

Insurance can play a role in protecting personal and business assets in the event of a successful lawsuit. Some types of liability insurance are mandated, such as workers' compensation or vehicle liability. There are specialized types of liability insurance, such as director and officer's liability and professional liability in the design, legal, or medical professions, for instance. Some types of businesses, such as construction, often require contractors to carry project completion insurance. This is not intended to be a complete recitation on the type or forms of insurance but rather another area where an insurance agency can provide coverage relative to your type of business.

Most startup businesses can't afford to buy all the coverage that they possibly could use, but as a general rule, a good commercial insurance agent can help you make these decisions to cover the most likely risks with the premium dollars you can afford. Coverage should focus on losses or claims that could wipe you out or at least severely damage you financially. Don't buy coverage, unless legally mandated, where a loss, if it happened, might hurt but wouldn't seriously financially wound you. In that instance, you are self-insuring.

Speaking of self-insuring, if your business eventually succeeds beyond your wildest dreams and becomes a very large organization, you might consider self-insuring. In my case, we decided to form a professional liability insurance company in Burlington, Vermont, and over the decade and a half that followed, we saved a very substantial amount of money. In fact, when I recapitalized our business, it was worth more than some of our operating companies.

Just as in personal lines of insurance, commercial insurance companies are not created equal when it comes to their financial strength, competitiveness of their rates, the quality of advice and service they provide, and the likelihood when push comes to shove that they will pay a fair claim.

You likely won't work with the agent you typically do for your personal insurance policies. Those are retail products, rather than commercial coverage. You need specialized expertise to know the type of commercial coverage you need—and can afford—to fit the risks inherent in your business, as well as evaluate insurance providers.

An unfortunate fact of commercial insurance is that some carriers are prone to deny coverage and litigate, rather than pay a bona fide claim. Their business practices suggest a business model based on denying claims, forcing the insured to litigate—when some won't be able to afford the cost and delayed payment—and settling for less, later. So be aware.

The next chapter will present some ideas on how to win and keep your buyers in delivering what you are in business to provide.

— CHAPTER 8 —

DELIVERING THE GOODS AND SERVICES

Most entrepreneurs start their business with the knowledge and experience to produce or provide the product or service at the heart of their business. If this isn't the case, it's not a franchise, and they don't bring in another party with that knowledge and experience, the chances of success significantly diminish. This chapter assumes you, the entrepreneur, have this base covered. Instead, this chapter will discuss other aspects of delivering goods and services particular to your business to influence your company's success.

COMMUNICATIONS

Successful businesses have to satisfy their customers and, as much as possible, do so every time. Satisfied customers are often repeat customers. It's hard for any business to survive, let alone grow, without repeat customers. Having a satisfied customer entails not only providing them with their desired product or service, when they want it, and for a price they think is fair—and all these things count, but doing so in a way that involves little hassle, ensuring a positive experience. For businesses that interact with their customers via the telephone or Internet, this can present both challenges and opportunities. Successful businesses strive for a welcoming, easy experience that makes customers or clients want to return. Most businesses conduct at least some of their customer contact through either the Internet—and there will be even more as time goes on—or the phone, as well as in person. We all have experienced the opposite. It doesn't have to be that way. Amazon is a classic case of a customer-friendly web interface. It's easy to find what you're looking for, purchase it, and return it, if necessary. I was surprised recently when I used the Social Security Administration's website for it, too, was very user-friendly. We can all think of examples that are the opposite. I just recently changed my bank because their online banking app was so difficult to use, and they required me to set up a new password every three months.

For successful companies, the quality and quantity of their communications are as important as the quality of their product or service.

If your business significantly depends on an Internet connection, I encourage you to invest where needed to ensure it creates the right image and encourages customers to choose business with you, rather than a competitor. Before you launch your website and interface with potential customers, I encourage you to beta-test it on a sample of your intended customers. If you own a retail business working with the general public, make sure your customers over the age of 40 find it a satisfying experience. I think in many cases the designers of these sites grew up with the technology of the web and don't recognize that many users are neophytes.

Although many businesses work hard to educate or force their customers to conduct business with them via the web, there are still a significant amount of businesses that, at least in part, depend on communicating with their customers and suppliers via telephone. We all are familiar with the automated answering systems that most businesses use. When you call, you first are told to listen carefully, "for our prompts have changed," and then you are informed your call is being recorded—whether you want it or not—for *training* purposes. Also, no matter the time of day, you hear an apology for "high call volume." They funnel you through a series of choices—do you need the billing department, the purchasing department, the warehouse, etc.?—and maybe there is an option that acknowledges you really need to talk to a human being. We understand why this happens: the technology is inexpensive and readily available, and it gives the appearance of saving labor costs. All of this may be true, yet for some businesses, it has the undesirable effect of irritating potential customers. I suspect some of us are a bit shocked and pleasantly surprised when we call and find a live person with a pleasant demeanor who seems eager to help us. Even in your startup days, I suggest you relay calls to someone's mobile phone when no one is available to answer the main number. At the very least, manage to leave a pleasant and welcoming message, giving the caller assurances that voicemails are routinely monitored and will be responded to in a certain timeframe—and then be sure you follow through with your promise. If someone is routinely assigned to answer your business phone, hopefully, that someone has that natural ability to make the caller feel they were just waiting for their call, rather than the caller feeling that somehow they interrupted the person's day and sort of wished they hadn't called. This is not a trivial issue. You want those who call to feel heard, appreciated, and valued. A little training goes a long way to accomplish this goal.

Written communications also influence your prospective employee's, customer's, and supplier's perception of your business. This is true for the sales side as well as with customer services when handling requests and complaints. If necessary, train your personnel who use written communications; it will pay dividends in building repeat business and help you create a positive image. Attention to detail matters—grammar, spelling, arithmetic, color scheme, graphics, and packaging, if part of your delivery system. All make a difference in how people, your customers, view you.

If your employees are uniformed, establish procedures to ensure that color, style, cleanliness, consistency, and professionalism represent your business in the best light. If you use automobiles or trucks with your company's name on them, make sure they are kept clean and well-maintained. I remember, during a visit to Tokyo, seeing a sanitation crew, all in spotless white uniforms, emptying a septic tank into a clean white tank truck. If this kind of business can do it, anyone can.

If your business entails preparing reports or other written communications, my experience suggests that when delivering a draft—often at the customer's insistence—it needs to demonstrate the same quality as the final report. No matter the caveats you give your customer to the effect that arithmetic, grammar, and spelling will be fixed before the report is finalized, a rough draft document that really is rough in that regard creates a poor impression regarding the quality of your work.

Paying attention to the means and quality of customer communications to and from your business will pay dividends in creating an image in which your employees take pride and your customers want to do business.

Another item to consider when you look at written or electronic communications, which may seem obvious but is often overlooked, is your target audience. One size seldom fits all. If you communicate with technical people, purchasing agents, salespeople, or senior management, it makes a difference. Each of these audiences typically has different priorities. For instance, technical people may want figures, options, and insights into your methods, whereas senior management may want the bottom line and the final product.

QUALITY

Quality assurance and quality control (QA/QC) are important to your communications. They are also important in the other aspects of the business. Most of us initially associate QA/QC with our work product, and that is appropriate. Satisfied customers expect you to deliver the quality they think they're purchasing. The QA/QC principles apply in your human resources arena, your IT department, accounting, warehousing, etc. One of the features of successful firms in the long run is quality and continuous improvement that is deeply embedded in the culture of the business. It gets that way best when it's built in from the beginning.

Many books and online resources are available that provide in-depth coverage on establishing QA/QC programs for different sizes and types of businesses. If you or one of your employees lacks knowledge and experience in this arena, it is worth the effort to obtain it. It will probably increase the odds that your business becomes a growing success story.

Satisfaction surveys are a frequently used tool for all kinds of businesses. This tool can be part of your QA/QC program. The mechanism may be part of your online Internet or phone connection with your customer or by old-fashioned mail. The likelihood of receiving critical feedback from the customer is greater if an independent third party ensures their responses remain anonymous. We all love compliments but are not quite so fond of criticism. However, it's a rare business indeed that, at all times and in all instances, leaves its customers completely satisfied. If you want to outcompete others and grow your customer base, one key element is to identify where you missed the mark and then fix it. It's safe to assume that everything isn't up to snuff if you receive negative feedback in certain areas from numerous customers. Recognize this is an opportunity that you might not have been aware of otherwise. Continuous improvement is part of the lifeblood of a successful company.

Previous chapters discussed some of the supposedly tangential aspects of delivering products or services. Contributors to the overall success of your business, however, include so much more—your personal ability, drive, personality, values, experience, the quality and attitudes of your employees, your location, culture, and business practices. The list could go on and on. All of these affect the success of your business.

PROBLEM CUSTOMERS

Unfortunately, you don't have to be a very big business or be in business very long to experience dealing with unhappy customers. Losing an unhappy customer is bad enough, but often, that customer will share their experience with others, ultimately costing you additional business. As tempting as it is to respond in a defensive manner, do your best to resist that impulse. Successful businesses adhere to the old adage "the customer is always right." Even when it's not true, still treat it as though it is. Many times, customer complaints are indeed legitimate. In this case, it's easier to accept the consequences and remedy the situation, which also implies looking internally to identify why this occurred and which procedures, if any, need to be implemented to ensure it doesn't repeat. Even when the complaint seems illegitimate, fixing it, on average, produces the best outcome.

The next chapter will discuss how to create and manage the growth of your business.

— CHAPTER 9 —

CREATING AND MANAGING GROWTH

STRATEGIC PLANNING

Substantial, sustained growth doesn't just usually happen. It is the result of long-range strategic planning underpinned by annual operating plans that, step by step, guide the business in implementing the strategic plan. The strategic plan—arguably THE key to long-term success—lays out what you want to achieve and the major strategic means of accomplishing it. Many books have been written on this subject. Unfortunately, time and space constraints limit what I can share in this book.

Many businesses recognize the value of planning but make the process so cumbersome as to be almost counterproductive. As an entrepreneur, you, ideally, should provide the initiative to produce this plan and update it periodically to accommodate changing circumstances. The simpler the plan, the better—and the more likely it will actually guide the growth of the business. My initial strategic plan was only a couple of pages. It guided ERM's growth for the first 10 years. When I felt it was imperative to expand internationally, my strategic plan was only six pages. It was the roadmap that guided the next 10 years. I might add that, initially, I wasn't able to convince some of my domestic partners that this was the best way to continue growing our business. It took a few years for them to see the benefits of an international reach to their domestic business.

There are various planning tools to consider in developing annual operating plans. ERM successfully used the Balanced Scorecard (check it out on the Web at balancedscorecard.org), which provided the means for us to ensure that individual employees understood their specific goals and responsibilities in implementing the overall strategic plan.

As mentioned, I found planning is most effective when it's both a top-down and a bottom-up exercise. It's a team effort. Everyone needs to understand the goal, the plan, and their role to make it happen.

CREATING GROWTH

Your strategic plan contains the major strategies you plan to implement to grow your business. In the next few pages, I outline some basic alternative routes for you to consider their applicability for your business.

DECENTRALIZE

In my business, and perhaps for you, the solution was to decentralize growth by starting new businesses and continually adding new products and services to existing businesses, with champions in each and every instance. For example, let's assume you have 100 employees in a service business, and they all work in one location, producing the same services. To grow 60 percent in a year, you need to grow your existing revenue sufficient to add 60 new employees. (In this simple example, I presume revenue is directly proportional to the number of employees. In real life, this isn't usually the case.)

Another way to achieve the same result is to start three new offices in geographically different markets. Let's say two existing employees in each of these new offices sell enough in the first year to need and hire ten new employees. Note, the smaller the business, all factors being equal, the easier it is to grow at a higher annual rate. As an example, if an entrepreneur starts a business as the only employee and, over the first year, generates enough new sales to add three employees and each of those employees generates the same revenue, then the business has grown 300 percent. The original office can sell enough work in their previously established service areas to require 15 new staff. Next, start three new service offerings in the original office. The three new service offerings added enough new business to require another 15 employees. In this way, you have grown your total business from 100 to 160 employees. That's a 60 percent increase in personnel, with a substantial increase in revenue, presuming hires were only made to support new business.

DIVERSIFY

What additional products or services do your existing clients and customers need that you could provide by adding additional capacity? It's a well-known fact that the easiest sale to make is to sell again something you've previously sold to an existing customer. The next easiest sale is to sell a new product or service to an existing customer. Following this logic, the hardest sale is for a product or service to someone you haven't previously done business with. If your customer is another business, institutional buyer, or government agency, do they need the same product or service in another division or location? Your existing customer can help you identify their counterparts, perhaps even offering a recommendation. So I ask again, does your customer need a product or service you could provide, bringing to bear additional resources? The same general principles apply to consumer-oriented businesses. See Figure 6.

Figure 6: Keys to Rapid Growth

EXPAND GEOGRAPHICALLY

For many businesses, their geographic footprint influences the size of their market and their ability to reach customers. That's why some businesses choose to use the Internet, sales agents, or representatives to extend their geographical reach. Another way is to establish your own presence in markets rich with opportunities. This strategy is particularly relevant when you supply a personal service, equipment rental, warehouse, or some other type of business that requires reasonable proximity to your customer. Most businesses have competitors, and some practical limits exist to the percentage of available business you can get in any one geographical market. Establishing (or acquiring) offices, divisions, or affiliates in different geographical regions is another way to obtain customers. Some businesses use the Internet to extend their geographical market. The geographical region for a business, such as a community bank or a dry cleaner, may be only a few miles, whereas for a more specialized business, with fewer potential customers, the reach might include multiple states or even the world.

In my case, as mentioned earlier, the strategy was to expand geographically in major regional markets in the United States, initially through establishing a single office in that region. In each case, these offices offered the same services to the same type of clients—primarily Fortune 500 companies. The next step was to add additional services initially in one region, and as we built staff and clientele in that new service area, we then added those same services to other regional businesses. Our next move was to start new companies—sister businesses in each region—providing complementary services, such as construction services to clean hazardous waste sites, analytical laboratory services, environmental drilling businesses that focused on defining groundwater and soil contamination, a catastrophic risk assessment business, a temporary staffing business to provide environmental specialists to other companies, and an environmental regulations information subscription business. Collectively, this created a substantial engine for growth. The growth was decentralized and therefore, in some ways, easier to achieve and easier to manage and staff. Part of the key to growing this fast without debt financing was developing exceptionally profitable businesses, thus creating the necessary working capital to grow further.

ACQUISITIONS

Another way to grow rapidly is to acquire other businesses. Through acquisitions, you can gain new geographical markets, technology, products, services, and customers. Besides the financial resources, successful growth via this mechanism requires management skills to make two plus two equal four or five, not three. A strategic acquisition can accelerate growth. My company acquired a relatively small but well-regarded environmental consulting firm in the UK in the 1980s as a base to build affiliated companies throughout Europe. This firm had also established a foothold in the far east with a profitable small office, which served as a springboard to set up and acquire other consulting firms in the Asia-Pacific global market. In each case, these new affiliates were partially owned by their local partners, just as in the United States, with the exception that the U.S. founding partners retained the majority interest.

The conceptual strategy I used to grow a global service business is not, alas, an original idea. Although I wasn't aware of it at the time I started, Ben Franklin set up a number of printing businesses along the east coast and Caribbean in the 1700s using a similar strategy. So did J.C. Penney in establishing an enormous partnership and later a corporation with key managers in over 800 stores throughout the United States. Common elements also existed in a number of law firms, real estate companies, and a life-care business in which I was a partner. This concept for growth can be used by many businesses. Might it be adopted for yours, too?

In many business sectors, "local" types of businesses, such as car washes, veterinarian practices, barber shops, and auto repair facilities are purchased—often by an entrepreneur who initially built a small business in one of these areas with borrowing or financial backing from investors.

The strategy I used to grow my business was spectacularly successful; however, like most good strategies, it was not necessarily the best forever. Our customers increasingly demanded to purchase global services for their operating units. Our structure was not optimal to meet that demand. Converting to a single legal entity that owned all or a controlling interest in our regional operating businesses was a better competitive structure at this stage of the then 24-year-old business. This necessitated a restructuring and convincing a lot of my reluctant partners to exchange their holdings in their regional companies for equity in the whole enterprise. My point is that it is very difficult to devise a strategy and structure that is extraordinarily successful in rapidly growing a successful business that is also optimal for a much larger business when the market changes—another consideration to keep in mind as you develop your growth strategy.

FRANCHISE

Everyone is familiar with the franchise business model. This option opens another avenue for geographical growth if your business can be standardized and you can build an attractive brand. In this case, you sell a franchisee the right to run a duplicate of your original business, usually in a specified geographical area. You provide a complete package of services and materials to the franchisee—usually with very specific directions on every phase of the business. Besides the original purchase price, the franchisee typically pays you a fee based on sales. Many different types of businesses have been and will be set up using this model.

LICENSING

For businesses that produce software or copyrighted material or promote endorsements using entertainment and sports personalities, authors, and others who create intellectual property, licensing their "products" is a very common way to grow revenue. Sometimes, an operating business's brand can become a merchandisable property in and of itself (think Trump). Licensing of brand names can produce significant income with little associated expenses.

THE DIGITAL WORLD

Many new entrepreneurs launch their businesses in the digital world. These businesses are typically inherently high-risk but also can be highly rewarding. They are also capable of scaling almost exponentially. My former group of companies also contained a digital business to help customers track state- and national-level environmental regulations and manage their corporate environmental data.

Today, commerce of all types is enmeshed (and many are dependent) to one degree or another on the "digital world." It is the modern equivalent of the industrial revolution. A "Siri" search on my iPhone for the number of commercial apps turned up a recent blog by Michael Fortin that stated there were over 35 million application titles with greater than 175 million application versions. As mind-boggling as that number is, in addition, the Google Play Store and the iOS App Store have an additional estimated 2.6 and 2.1 million apps, respectively. Still, there are opportunities to utilize the Web to develop better tools or additional tools to meet human wants and needs.

MANAGING GROWTH

I know you might say, "That's the least of my worries. I'm trying to get growth. I don't need to worry about managing it." Before we launch into this, a word of caution. Believe it or not, too much growth can be as bad as too little. During my business career, I led two service companies at sustained growth rates of over 60 percent per year. On one hand, this is terrific, but on the other, it put a lot of strain on the company's infrastructure, staff, and capital base. You need to be very profitable to sustain that type of growth (as in my case) or have lenders and investors willing to sustain this type of growth for the long-term return. Very rapid growth can affect your ability to maintain quality, meet schedules, and obtain additional equipment, space, and personnel at an appropriate pace. There are ways in which you can grow very rapidly and minimize these problems.

As your business grows, you need to know what to keep and what to change. Growth brings increasing demands on management, staff, systems, equipment, and finances. As humans, we tend to resist change, sometimes to our detriment. It's easier for people to accept change in small increments than to accommodate wholesale changes overnight. Change is inherent to thrive over time.

As much as you can, make incremental changes. This also has an advantage because not every incremental change will work better than the old way. It's less disruptive to undo a small change and a different tactic than when making major changes.

Change can create new opportunities for your staff. In the long run, changes can attract and keep good people, but at times, it can also create challenges when their jobs outgrow the person. It's tempting to solve this challenge by simply letting that person go and hiring or promoting someone else. That may in fact be the best decision. However, it also is a loss for the company when the individual has been an outstanding employee in the past. If possible, try training, coaching, rearranging some job responsibilities, or reassignment. If that doesn't work, it can be a problem for both you and the employee. One of the common mistakes I made was promoting a great doer into a manager's job. There are obvious reasons why this is the natural next step, and when it's successful, it is a win for both parties. However, an outstanding salesperson, as an example, is not necessarily even an average manager of other salespeople. The job requires a different set of skills. When it doesn't work, you lose not only a manager but, in some cases, an outstanding salesperson.

I'm sure there are other types of businesses that I haven't touched upon, other growth strategies that may be applicable to your business, and some other way to deal with the challenges of growth, but the ones I cover here and in other chapters can also be part of a winning formula. If you think about your business and your expansion goals, would one or more of these strategies work for you?

When it is all said and done, making a profit is—at best—what it is all about. Stay tuned for more on this in the next chapter.

— CHAPTER 10 —

MAKING A PROFIT

For many entrepreneurs, but not all, the principal reason they go into business is to make a profit. On the surface, it looks pretty straightforward—sell your product or service for more than it costs you to build or execute it, and you should make a profit. In some ways that just sums it up. In reality, however, it's more complicated and certainly more difficult.

The first decision for the entrepreneur is to determine how important it is to make a profit. For some, profitability is a secondary or even tertiary reason to start a business. For some, it's more about fame and visibility; for others, it's supposedly about the freedom of working for yourself. For another subset, it's more of an escape from other factors in their lives. In the end, every business ultimately needs to make enough money to stay in business. Making a profit is what the so-called "free enterprise" system is all about. In my experience, the owner's attitude and desire substantially contribute to the profitability of the business. Staying significantly and consistently profitable doesn't just happen—*the probability of profitability increases significantly when the business makes quality, customer service, and profitability major elements of everyone's job—part of the cultural foundation of the business.*

Profits are not only desired by entrepreneurs as a return on their investment in the business and a reward for the risks; they are also usually necessary to grow the business. I recognize that we are in an era of startups, especially in the e-commerce sector, where some entrepreneurs grow rich by growing rapidly, without profits, through either debt, venture capital, or both. For most businesses, this isn't usually an option. It must be done the old-fashioned way, by growing *and* making a profit. For my former company, ERM, profitability was key to funding extraordinary growth. Some of ERM's regional companies consistently achieved 30-plus percent pretax profit margins annually on net revenue.

For service businesses that derive their income from the labor of those who provide the services, there is a simple, but rather elegant, formula that depicts the interrelationship:

$$P=1 - 1/MUR$$

P represents profits as a percentage of net revenues (excluding subcontractors and reimbursable expenses, if any); M is the multiplier on raw compensation (without benefits); U equals utilization of labor (i.e., direct raw compensation—the labor directly involved in providing the service—divided by the business's total raw compensation); and R represents the salary-to-expense ratio (i.e., total raw compensation divided by total expenses, excluding reimbursable expenses, if any). As an example, for a service firm, if we assume $M = 3.0$, $U = 0.65$, and $R = 0.65$, then the pre-tax profit is the following:

$$P=1 - 1/(3.0 \times .65 \times .65) = 0.21, \text{ or } 21\%$$

You can also calculate what the multiplier on direct labor has to be to meet your profit target when you know your expense ratio.

MARKUP

Competition usually limits the markup that the market will bear on direct labor or the cost to produce a product. You can push that limit with customers that value quality and service if you ensure you deliver both of those, but there still is a limit. Therefore, you have two ways to improve profitability: one is to reduce your indirect overhead costs, which include all labor and expenses not typically involved in generating income, and the second is to improve productivity. The first implies a tight watch on labor and expenses not directly serving customers. The second is staying abreast of new innovations or technology to reduce costs in any and all parts of the business.

Of course, there are other ways to increase profitability in some situations, such as delivering services on a lump sum or fixed-price basis, IF your price is competitive enough to win AND you can deliver the desired results with less total costs. Another contracting strategy that CAN yield above-market profit may work when the services provided create measurable savings and you can contractually share the savings for a defined period.

Service businesses have the advantage of little, if any, inventory. They also typically have less need for working capital because there is less time between when they pay expenses and receive payment by customers. There are notable exceptions to this, for example, medical practices that rely on third-party payment (government or insurance companies).

Inventory can be a profit killer. It's particularly an issue with businesses that work with materials or products with a very short shelf life.

Businesses that are built on fashion or furnishings, where styles and tastes have short life cycles, are especially exposed to this risk, as well as businesses that focus on seasonal goods and services. An example of the latter is a snowmobile dealership or rental that carries inventory for a snowy winter that doesn't materialize. I know because I was a partner in a marina business dependent on a warm, dry summer season and adequate snowfall when snowmobiles were added as a winter business.

OVERHEAD

Most entrepreneurs, when starting a business, are quite thrifty with minimal overhead costs. As time passes, however, with human nature what it is, we accumulate activities and costs that contribute marginally, if at all, to the main goals of the business. Some of this happens as a business grows and becomes a more complex organization. It requires additional diligence to track operations and nurture your original culture. In many cases, we address this creeping overhead when forced by a downturn in our sales. When we notice our profits shrink, it provides the incentive we require to clean house.

As your business grows, so too does the complexity of your organizational structure. Many businesses adopt a profit center organizational structure, where the company's total business may be divided into units that correspond to geographical markets, types of products or services, customers, or other logical configurations. Individual business units or profit centers then accumulate their own overhead. When the profit center has its own profit-and-loss accounting, this provides the business unit with more control over their overhead. However, one of the drawbacks of this organizational structure is it can result in people and functions that don't necessarily optimize the overall performance of the total business. Also, the home office corporate group of staff employees usually provides services to the overall company and the individual profit centers. As a result, corporate management often devises a methodology to allocate the corporate overhead to individual profit centers. This is almost always a source of friction and conflict between the operating units or profit centers and the company's corporate management. Profit center managers often feel they don't get their money's worth; they're not given a choice of the services they want and therefore resist paying for them. In a way, this is a healthy situation because it tends to put pressure on minimizing unnecessary overhead costs, which serves everybody's interests. If you are just starting your business, as I mentioned earlier, this is not going to be your immediate concern. If your objective is to become a larger business, it probably will be.

BUDGETS

Budgets are powerful tools, helping management to grow profitably. In fact, budgets are a plan to produce profits. I found that a combination of bottom-up and top-down produces the best results in developing an annual budget. In my case, this meant that each profit center manager asked his staff to help prepare income targets and expense budgets for the coming year. The top-down side usually provided aspirational targets to cover the total business, as well as new investments and overhead staff functions. Sometimes it's a hard balancing act to encourage growth through aspirational or stretch income (sales) targets while at the same time maintaining realistic goals with a better than 50 percent chance of achieving them. This top-down and bottom-up approach usually required several cycles before locking in on a final set of numbers.

A budget should be a living document. Accounting systems should show income and expenses (by profit center, if in place) each month compared to the budget. Again, variances in either sales or expense categories are subject to discussion, and when appropriate, the budget should change to account for unexpected significant changes in sales. If necessary, reduce future expense budgets for the desired results in the following month(s). In this way, you make a plan, and then you work the plan with all parties involved.

Each individual is "wired" differently. The spectrum includes those with cautious temperaments to those who are over-optimistic. Ideally, try to avoid both ends of this gambit. Good accounting systems provide a framework for good budgeting. Even in the startup and early years of building a business, there is just no substitute for good budget and accounting practices.

CASH MANAGEMENT

Cash management is also an important discipline to develop. Most budgets are usually crafted assuming accrual accounting, as are profit and loss income statements. This methodology gives an accurate picture of the health of the business, but it doesn't represent your cash position. That requires a cash accounting approach. If the income statement is assembled by month, showing income as cash is received and expenses are actually paid, then the bottom line shows whether your cash position is growing or shrinking. By adding another line at the bottom that shows starting cash at the beginning of the month, and each month that follows is added or subtracted as appropriate, then you can monitor a running total of your cash position at the end of each month. Your income statements on an accrual basis can show great profitability, but if your cash depletes faster than customers pay you, you can find yourself struggling to stay in business. This is a not an uncommon way for businesses to fail.

Cash profits are crucial to fuel the working capital that growth requires. If your business on average is paid within 30 days, you will require working capital of at least one month's expenses—exclusive of capital purchases. If your sales grow at 12 percent per year (or approximately 1 percent per month), your working capital needs to increase by at least 1 percent (less profit) each month. Therefore, you will need to retain after-tax profits of at least 12 percent in the business to avoid borrowing.

If you, as the owner of this hypothetical business, want to spend some of the profits, you either need to increase profitability, receive payments quicker, reduce growth, or borrow. Hopefully, you can substitute your budget or actual figures to see the interrelationship between growth, profitability, and working capital in your business.

Notice that working capital requirements directly relate to the length of time your business incurs cash expenses for work in progress and the time you receive cash for your product or service. (Working capital is the difference between current assets and current liabilities.) To minimize working capital, businesses purchase on extended terms, order as close to usage as possible, and receive payment in advance or as soon as they can. To know your business's working capital requirements, you need to consider both sides of this coin. For instance, inventory of parts or finished goods increases working capital needs. Some buying sectors are often slow to pay. One of those sectors is often government.

Three other ratios entrepreneurs need to be familiar with are current ratio, debt coverage, and debt to equity. The current ratio is a measure of near-term liquidity and is determined by dividing current accounts receivable by current accounts payable. The result should be greater than one. The more the ratio exceeds one, the better. Debt coverage is a measure of the business's ability to stay current with debt repayment. It is calculated by dividing annual after-tax cash flow by annual debt service payments (principal and interest). Again, that ratio needs to be at least one. Lenders want to see something greater to provide a margin of safety. The debt-to-equity ratio is used to measure the relative percentage of the shareholder equity used to finance the company. This is calculated by dividing the total debt by shareholders' equity. The resulting ratio is an indication of the degree of leverage. The higher the leverage, the greater the risk of default.

You probably recognize that one of the limiting factors in how successful your business is or will be is you. Your knowledge, skills, experience, and contacts can be increased and, as a result, increase the success of your business. What is your plan to improve your knowledge, skill, and contact base? Additional information in this area will be covered in the next chapter.

— CHAPTER 11 —

GROWING YOUR ABILITY TO SUCCEED

Most successful entrepreneurs want to learn how to be even more successful entrepreneurs. In fact, if you chose to read this book, this is likely your desire, too. This chapter will touch on several means of accomplishing that success. The starting point in this regard is to realize you'll never know as much as you could benefit from knowing, and you need to be willing to continually add to your knowledge and experience.

SELF EDUCATION

To gain more knowledge in specific subjects and areas, there are some fairly obvious resources. Consider the community college or university in your area. Many allow adults to audit classes with or without fees. In some instances, classes are available in the evenings or online. The traditional source of seeking knowledge through books—one of the best resources—is also still available. If you can't find it in the public library, try the Internet. For how-to instruction, watch YouTube videos. Many books come in an audio e-book format, which allows you the convenience to listen to the book while exercising, gardening, doing chores around your home, or, when safe, driving.

MENTORS

Another highly recommended way to improve yourself is to find a compatible and knowledgeable mentor. One source is SCORE (www.score.org), a national organization with chapters throughout the country that helps entrepreneurs find mentors.[12] Their pay is the satisfaction from helping you succeed. These are usually experienced businesspeople, and some are also entrepreneurs. You can contact this organization via the Internet at score.org. There may be other such organizations in your area, or you may have a personal relationship with someone willing to help you. This can be a rewarding experience for both parties, speaking from personal experience. I mentored an entrepreneur who started a small benefits insurance brokerage firm. I had the pleasure of working with him for a number of years and watching his organization grow to be one of the larger firms in our metropolitan area. I no longer mentor him, but we developed a personal friendship that continues 25 years later.

---

12 This organization is a great resource for entrepreneurs. It was started in 1964 and claims to have more than 11 million entrepreneurs. They offer onsite and web-based workshops, webinars, and an online library of resources, in addition to a national pool of experienced business mentors—almost all without charge.

MUTUAL-HELP ORGANIZATIONS

Membership in certain outside organizations can offer you opportunities to meet other entrepreneurs and business people. Some of these organizations provide formal programs designed to improve your knowledge, skill base, and/or contacts. One such organization is the Young Entrepreneurs' Organization. The qualifications, cost, and types of programs they sponsor are detailed on their website, which is https://hub.eonetwork.org/. For those of you with an organization large enough and young enough to qualify for the Young Presidents' Organization, this is an excellent source—again, speaking from personal experience—to help you grow both as a person and as an executive or business owner. Check this organization out on the Web at http://www.ypo.org for additional information. Several organizations provide in-person and/or online educational programs on a wide variety of subjects. One of the best-known is the American Management Association. You can check this organization's offerings on their website (www.amanet.org).

ADVISORY BOARD

An advisory Board of Directors is an invaluable aid in growing yourself and your business. As the name suggests, these individuals have no legal liability; their sole purpose is to help you succeed. It's never too early or too late to recruit a small group of people interested in lending their experience and advice. Think about people you know who might be willing to serve on your advisory board. Usually, such boards meet quarterly, but the frequency of meetings is completely at the discretion of you and your board members. Many times, individuals are willing to help, particularly at the startup stage, without expecting any compensation. Even if you feel it's appropriate to recognize the value of their time and advice, a nominal honorarium will usually suffice. People willing to fill this role don't do it because of the money but because they find satisfaction in helping you.

I know from firsthand experience. I have been serving for over 25 years on an advisory board for a firm that published (printed) around 30 newsletters covering human resources, sales, marketing, and safety, among other topics, and now, it is successfully converting to an all web-delivered product portfolio. Such a board should exclude family members, close personal friends, and paid outside advisors, such as your lawyer or accountant. I suggest excluding this group because it is more difficult to receive objective advice and, sometimes, advice you don't want to hear. Ideally, you can find people from different backgrounds with different strengths, such as marketing and sales, finance, human resources, legal, etc. You will benefit and learn from this advisory board, not only because of the advice you receive but also because they will minimize your blind spots inherent in all human beings.

You also need to organize and prepare for these meetings. This in itself often helps you "see better" how best to run your business or make specific decisions.

LEGAL BOARD

When your business grows to a certain size, a Board of Directors can be beneficial. In this case, people who join you as directors take on official fiduciary responsibilities and legal liability. To significantly reduce the risk these individuals take on, obtain directors' and officers' liability insurance. Criteria for selecting official directors is no different than that of advisory board members. With an advisory board, there are no consequences of refusing advice from your advisors; however, if this is a pattern, there's either something wrong with the advice you receive or with your thinking as the captain of your ship. With a legal board of directors, they assume the overarching responsibility for your business. The board typically hires, evaluates, and fires the chief executive officer (who might be you). The board usually approves certain types of actions by the company, such as borrowing, purchasing, or selling major assets over preset limits.

TIME MANAGEMENT

From my own experience, one of the big skills to master is managing your time. No matter who we are, we only get 24 hours a day, seven days a week, and a finite number of heartbeats in our lifetime. A starting point is to list your personal time priorities. Possible items on your list might include building a successful business. If it doesn't, then you probably should not start one. Other items on your list might include family time, exercise or sports, travel, civic and religious participation, reading, and self-improvement. Your list might include other hobbies for which you want to make time.

The likelihood of a successful outcome increases if you consciously prioritize and learn time-management skills. You might find it interesting and surprising to track your time by activity for a week. Pick a typical week on your calendar. Note on your mobile phone or on paper each time you switch from one category to another. Include the time you spend on categories not on your priority list, such as meals, sleeping, commuting, walking the dog, personal hygiene, talking to your neighbor, etc. When you total all the time spent on different activities during that week, how closely did that correspond to your personal priorities? For most of us, the answer is usually not so much. In hindsight, perhaps it wasn't a very typical week. More likely, if you conduct this exercise again, the individual activities will vary a lot, but the bottom line will remain the same—we typically don't spend our time the way we think we do or the way we want to.

If you do this exercise and reach a similar result, do you want to learn how to spend more of your time the way you hoped to—to better manage your time? A good place to start is to write down your major goals—what's most important in your life? Review the list of the ways you actually spent your time. How does it match up with your goals? For me, my primary life goals were to build a successful business, my family, have my wife and children rate me as a good husband and father, give back to my community, swim three times a week, see the world, and continue to learn. I attempted to organize my time to match. Life happens—most of us, no matter how hard we try, can only approach managing our time to meet each of our goals. My family and business goals were very difficult to accomplish simultaneously. However, I came closer to meeting my goals by consciously working at it than I otherwise would have. The same can be true for you.

One time-management technique that worked for me and many others is to make habitual lists, if you don't already. Numerous methods exist from time-management gurus, but this is the essence of mine. Each weekend, I wrote down the major goals I wanted to accomplish in the coming week. I prioritized them into must-do and hope-to-do. I compiled a second list of longer-term items—beyond next week—again divided into two categories. I reviewed my lists from the previous week and noted those I didn't accomplish (yes, there are always those items). If they were still relevant, I included them on the next week's list.

With my list in hand, I prioritized the must-do items and estimated the time it would take. This gave me a sense of how realistic my plan was. You learn from experience that others' need for your time—unexpected but usual interruptions—will take significant amounts of your time. If you don't allow for it, you will likely be frustrated at not being able to accomplish what *you* wanted to get done.

I tried to work the obvious business tasks around family time, kids' sporting events, my three swims a week, etc. I checked my list several times a day, crossed off items that I finished, added new ones, and sometimes eliminated others or changed priorities. In other words, my list was a living, changing guide for managing my time. Hopefully, some form of this tool will also help you accomplish more of the truly important aspects in your life. It will also help you decide what *not* to do—for me, it was playing golf on a regular basis due to the time it required.

If you have an assistant at work, inform them of your time plan. They can help you stick with it. If you have a mentor, or plan on getting one, again, share your time-management plan. Some of us have a partner or spouse that can not only help us in this area but also encourage a negotiation on time usage that they support. It's no secret that being an entrepreneur can put an additional strain on your personal relationships. If those relationships are important to you, be proactive in fostering them. The better you can achieve a satisfactory balance between your home life and your business, the more likely both will succeed.

One of the best investments I made over my career is to hire the best talent I could find as an administrative assistant, even during my initial startup months. If empowered to do so, they can substantially leverage your time to focus on tasks that matter the most.

It may seem like a stretch now, but don't dismiss the rest of the world in thinking about building your business. If this is of interest to you, read the next chapter.

— CHAPTER 12 —

GROWING INTERNATIONALLY

Depending on your business sector, there are many small businesses that sell to customers and, in some cases, even have offices or facilities outside of the United States. Even if you don't currently have international dealings, this chapter may inspire you to think of the longer-term possibilities of creating a business with international connections. If you offer a product or service with the potential to grow internationally, now or eventually, this chapter will provide an introduction.

The Internet has changed the world in many ways. This certainly includes commerce. The international market is not only a place to sell, but it is also a source of suppliers. For instance, the husband of one of my granddaughters subcontracted with an Indian software firm to perform some of the development work on one of his applications. At the moment, he's a one-person U.S.-based firm. Supplier networks are often global, and even very small companies find it to their advantage to leverage offshore procurement. The bottom line is if the nature of your business is such that suppliers, labor, or buyers could be situated offshore, you may be able to take advantage of the international market.

We previously covered marketing and sales, and generally, those same tools are applicable in offshore markets. Language is not the barrier that it once was. English is the language of business pretty much everywhere, particularly in Europe and the former Commonwealth of Nations. It's also an advantage to be able to conduct business in the local language. If you can bring that to bear, it's certainly a plus, but it's usually not essential.

Each country, and sometimes even within a country, has its own particular rules and regulations, similar to the United States. For instance, there may be unique import or export taxes to the goods or country with which you do business. Obviously, taxes (sales, value added, income) have to be verified wherever you happen to conduct business. Laws covering labor, liability, and privacy, for example, differ in many places from those in the United States. Be particularly cautious when conducting business in nondemocratic countries and in the developing economies of the world. Your contract may not be enforceable. These additional hurdles are not insurmountable obstacles, but they require attention. Another consideration is the currency in which you fulfill a transaction. Customary contract terms may differ, and currency fluctuations relative to the U.S. dollar pose additional risks.

Establishing a physical presence with staff can present a host of additional concerns, depending on the location, none of which are necessarily insurmountable. Labor laws in many cases are significantly different than in the United States. In most cases, in the States, as a non-union employer, you can hire and fire as you more or less wish, after accounting for gender, race, and age discrimination-type issues. In many offshore places, this is not the case. Employees in general and particularly in

Europe often have more rights than in the States. Separating employees once hired can be very difficult. Therefore, in many cases, employers use personnel not on their payroll. This is merely one example among others where a neophyte needs guidance from knowledgeable people about the particular country in which you plan to operate.

The pandemic of 2020-2021 accelerated the transition to working from home using Zoom and other similar Internet platforms. This also made it easier to utilize out-of-country staff without establishing offshore legal entities or offices. Another way to use international staff is through third parties, such as "People 2.0," who act as employer, agent, or administrator. This may be particularly attractive for short-term staffing needs.

It's never too early to think about your long-term goals, particularly in the context of when to exit your business. Some thoughts to consider are included in the next chapter.

— CHAPTER 13 —

EXITING YOUR BUSINESS

This chapter is likely more pertinent to those who started their business some time ago and are looking ahead to the time they will sell. For new entrepreneurs, it may seem strange as you focus on your start to talk about your exit. My experience, however, suggests that if you spend a little bit of time thinking about this subject at the beginning, it may affect decisions you make now that will be hard to undo later. You will have a number of options, one of which is to sell your business to family members. If that is an option for you, you should mention this to whomever advises you. There could be tax-advantage vehicles to accomplish this transition down the road if set up properly in the beginning. Selling to family members—for instance, a brother—might differ from selling to your children when it comes to valuing the business. If this is a possibility, considering it now can be very advantageous in the future. There are a lot of other factors that relate to this type of sale, but it's beyond the scope of this book.

Another exit strategy for entrepreneurs is to sell to partners. This transition can be set up with a buy-sell arrangement in the beginning, and it can take many forms. The third option is to sell to employees. Employee stock ownership plans (ESOP) can accomplish this. Federal tax law makes it possible to transfer ownership to employees through an employee stock ownership plan with tax advantages for the entrepreneur. It is one of the ways that the U.S. government encourages employee ownership of businesses. This vehicle can be used by all sorts of businesses and all sizes. When it became time for me to exit, I considered several options, including this one. In my case, this route was ultimately turned down by my partners who planned to stay. Their decision was driven primarily by wanting to preserve the status quo—including to keep me working. This was not surprising. We humans resist change. Ultimately, I found another route—a leveraged partial buyout by an outside, large, publicly traded investment firm based in the UK that won my partners' approval.

Many companies are ultimately sold to outside buyers. A competitor may absorb your business or operate it as a semi-independent entity, or it can be sold to investors. Buyers may want your management to stay in place, including you for a period of time. They may want to bring in top management of their choice or some combination of the two. Some buyers look to acquire a company to operate themselves. Sometimes, competitors want to buy your customer base, your product line, service, or technology. In some instances, it's a vertical integration, such as one of your suppliers buying your company as a means of increasing their distribution channels.

Another increasingly common alternative in many business sectors occurs when investors consolidate small- and medium-sized companies into a larger organization that they then sell to an even larger organization or take it public. This type of buyer often can bring economies of scale to improve profitability or expand products or services through the businesses they acquire. For instance, one of my adult children recently sold their multi-doctor veterinary practice to an entity that had acquired a number of other, similar clinics.

Investment-type buyers come in all sizes and forms, ranging from individuals who wish to play an active role in the business to very large, publicly traded funds. When I exited from my company, as I mentioned, the buyer was a publicly traded investment company on the London Stock Exchange, which held equity stakes in a couple of thousand different businesses in different sectors operating in different parts of the world.

You could take your company public with a listing on one of the stock exchanges. This is usually limited to reasonably good-sized companies, but there are exceptions, particularly if your business is an extremely fast-growing business in a popular sector with investors. If you elect this option, the owners of the business will probably be able to sell only a small percentage of their ownership at the public offering and will be required to hold the remaining equity for a period of time. A whole book could be written on this subject alone; the purpose here is only to raise the curtain on a long-term objective to monetize your hard work and good fortune.

In some cases, business owners decide to simply shut it all down. If this is done for reasons other than bankruptcy, where creditors "own" any remaining salvage value, then you should consider the possibility of selling intangible assets, such as your customer list, name (or brand), or patents with potential value to another party.

Another fact of life in selling a business is size matters. In general, the bigger the business, the higher the multiple of earnings the seller is likely to receive. Size also influences the type of potential buyers. Large investment funds and institutional buyers typically only seek businesses of significant size—perhaps $50 million to $100 million in sales. There are many exceptions to this, especially in "hot" or very fast-growing business niches, such as in the e-commerce area, or in more ordinary areas, like car wash businesses, for example. According to *The Wall Street Journal*, private equity buy-out firms in the United States owned more than 10,000 companies, as of June 30, 2022; 80 percent of these companies had valuations between $25 million and $1 billion.[13]

Selling a business is an art, not a science. However, one of the better approaches, and one that I used in selling my last business in 2016, utilized the following process. As a first step, start preparing your business for sale three to five years before you intend to pull the trigger. During that time, if your business wasn't using an outside accounting firm to prepare at least reviewed statements, do so now. Clean up your financial records—collect or write off doubtful receivables and extract the company from litigation, if any. Growth in sales and profits will be a major factor in determining the value of your business. Develop confidence in your projections of future sales and profits by doubling down on making each year's actual results meet or beat your budgets for the year leading up to a sale. Thoroughly rid the business of extraneous activities and costs. Do your best to see that key staff are in place and will likely stay post-sale. If possible, have a replacement for yourself in the wings, even if the buyer wants you to stay. Avoid, where possible, long-term leases and fixed costs, which will limit a buyer's flexibility.

A year before you want to sell, locate an advisor to help you find a buyer that meets your goals, which could include a commitment to

---

13 Ziati Meyer, "The Week in Numbers: August 20-21," Wall Street Journal, August 26, 2022, URL.

retain your employees for a specific time, the timeframe you want to continue working, the price you want, etc. The "right" advisor will have a lot of previous experience, preferably with your type of business, a large database of potential buyers, personal chemistry that works for you, references that check out, responsiveness, and a counseling ability and genuine desire to help you achieve your goals in addition to their fee.

Large organizations, such as Generational Equity and BCMS Capital, sponsor one-day seminars in major cities around the country on the selling process. I attended both firms' seminars and found them very worthwhile and fairly free from pressure to use them as your advisor. They both provide selling services through a network of linked individuals scattered across the United States.

Many small local and regional firms use the same tools and methods as the national firms. Some specialize in particular areas, such as retail, service, or logistics. Many are generalists. Some represent only sellers while others only buyers, but most represent both. There are also business brokers who, for the most part, operate similarly to those who sell private homes.

You will need to expend time and energy to find the "right" advisor. This can be a bit tricky because most sellers don't want to prematurely reveal plans to sell to their customers or employees. You don't want employees to leave, fearing the change in ownership, or lose customers when competitors suggest you may not be around. You may have contacts in your industry to discreetly query for possible agents. Your business attorney, banker, or outside tax accountant may be helpful. Talk to others you know who have sold their business and who will keep your inquiry confidential.

When I recently went through this process to sell a company that originally was part of the ERM Group, I considered several advisors, who had different fee structures. In all cases, the ultimate fee I would incur was a function of the selling price. You can make an approximate comparison by assuming a sale price and calculating the fee each advisor planned to charge. This is, of course, only one factor to consider, but my advice is to make it a minor one. It's more important to pick the advisor you think will do the best job for you.

When selling your business, you want multiple buyers to compete, rather than setting a price and trying to find a buyer. This is one of the differences in selling a business versus your home. A home realtor typically negotiates with you on the listing price and is bound by ethics and law to bring you any purchase offer they receive. It's up to you to decide to accept, counter, or reject, with or without advice from your realtor. Home realtors maximize their income by turning over sales as quickly as possible. They are not necessarily motivated to get you the highest price, which may require substantially more of their time, advertising dollars, etc. With rare exceptions, in a *normal* housing market, which wasn't the case in 2021 and 2022, when supply and demand are in balance or supply is greater than demand, the seller will likely receive less than the original asking price.

The selling process with potential to maximize your results follows these basic steps:

1. You develop a restated, "adjusted" income statement that eliminates costs unique to current ownership, such as family, on the payroll with nominal job responsibilities, inclusion of family in benefit plans, automobiles, etc., and special perks you gave yourself or others. Adjust your salary and bonuses and perhaps that of family members to reflect actual market-based compensation. These "adjustments" can be material in increasing the

profitability of your business for a new owner. You will also have to defend these adjustments to an eventual buyer.

2. You develop a brief, five-to-20-page profile or teaser document of your business, including products/services, major customers by name or type of business, including a summary of your last three to five years of sales and "adjusted" income, plus a three-to-five-year forecast of future sales and earnings, your selling methodology, location(s), and management team. If confidentiality at this stage is crucial, you can avoid specifics that identify your business. Your agent should help you with this task, but you will need to do the bulk of the work.

3. In consultation with you, your agent will send this brief teaser document to as many potential buyers as possible.

4. Responding interested parties (hopefully at least 20 to 30) will be asked to sign a confidentiality agreement to receive a much more detailed "book" on your business. They may also be asked at this stage to indicate a price or dollar range that they might be willing to pay IF all the details check out.

5. You and your agent decide which of the responding parties you will invite to the next step. Ideally, five or six of the initial responders are attractive buyers.

6. The invited prospective buyers, after receiving the "book," are required to respond by a stated date with interest, if any, in

pursuing a purchase and a price and terms if there are no surprises when they do their "due diligence."

7. You and your agent evaluate the "offers"—hopefully all five or six—and decide which one represents the best fit per your goals, which may not be the highest dollar offer. Considerations of the terms as well as the amount may be very material—all cash at closing versus 60 percent cash—and the rest based on the next three years' earnings.

8. The selected buyer makes an on-site visit, interviews key staff, and conducts a detailed review of your financials, customers, sales records, legal issues, etc. At the conclusion of this step, they indicate if they will close on the terms they offered, more likely discount their offer based on information they learned during their due diligence, or not pursue the purchase. If it's the second option, you can reject this modified offer, accept it, or negotiate a deal.

9. If the deal falls through, you have the option of advising your second choice (whom you presumably haven't advised that you rejected their offer) and repeat steps seven and eight.

Sometimes, if this process doesn't yield the price, potential buyers, or predetermined criteria you want the first time, assuming a choice, you can try again at a later time.

Economic conditions in general and outside your control will affect the value and terms of a sale. A seller's market is always better than a buyer's market. One of my family members recently sold their business after reaching step eight and was unwilling to accept the potential buyer's last-minute discount. A year later, they repeated the whole process and closed at twice the price of the previous buyer with better terms. Persistence and patience can pay off handsomely.

Before closing this subject, a bit more on how buyers in a competitive environment typically value a business. Buyers are motivated by many factors—such as your "fit" with their acquisition strategy, quality of your staff, customers, technology, location(s), capital required, cash flow, etc., but the big draw is usually past and likely growth in sales and profits. Thus, in the end, the buyer is buying *future* value. All other factors reasonably equal, businesses with high growth rates will yield a premium—perhaps over 100 percent—over a like business with very modest single-digit growth rates.

It isn't possible to forecast earnings a business might expect without knowing all the specifics, including timing. To give you some idea, the range might be less than one, or over ten, times adjusted earnings. A typical—if there is such a thing—scenario for a business with $1 million to $10 million in sales and modest growth in a stable business sector might be three to five. When you interview potential advisors—I strongly encourage you to select at least three to compare—they may provide an educated guess of the value you might achieve. Keep in mind that the value of your business is not just an accounting exercise from a business appraisal. The methodologies used for that purpose might be based on a discounted cash flow of estimated future earnings, book value, comparative sales, or another accounting approach.

These other methods are sometimes used to value an estate for tax purposes or to value collateral for a loan. They may or may not have a close relationship to market value. The discounted cash flow approach assumes an arbitrary discount rate to apply to a future stream of cash flow or earnings from the business—say for the next five to ten years. The sum of those discounted future earnings plus book value provides an estimated value of the business. The discount recognizes the value of a dollar now is one, but the value of a future dollar is less. Book value—the difference between assets and liabilities—is usually a very conservative valuation. Comparative sales are often used to value residential real estate, for example.

When you decide to sell, many considerations are before you, such as the effect on employees and your customers, as well as your own financial well-being. Each entrepreneur will weigh these factors, among others, differently to ensure consistency with their own value system, needs, and circumstances.

The purpose of this book was to increase the likelihood that you build a successful business with longevity and, someday, if you're lucky enough, work your way through this process. My hope is that this book helps you accomplish your dreams.

— CHAPTER 14 —

SHARING SOME FINAL THOUGHTS

Throughout this book, I shared some of the key lessons from my business and personal life experiences. To recap, a successful business needs a clear vision, dynamic leadership, and a culture that values integrity, people and their contributions, risk-taking, excellence, continuous improvement, and a willingness to do whatever it legally and morally takes. You should encourage and promote candid and open communication, minimal bureaucracy and politics, fairness, and alignment of staff and company goals.

I want to leave you with some final observations. Most of us can do far more than we think we can. There is no substitute for effort. If you don't care, you can't motivate others to care. If you want something to count, you have to count it. If a "rough draft" product is given to a customer, it better not be a rough draft. If you give a customer an estimated cost along with a long list of caveats, you can count on two facts: they will remember the number, and they will forget the caveats. The perception of the passage of time is inversely proportional to the amount of time you unconsciously feel you have left—the older you are, and the less time you have left in this life, the faster time seems to pass.

One of the harder lessons I had to learn is the difference between effectiveness and efficiency. Compensation is important, but for most of us, it's a poor substitute for appreciation and recognition. If you want more joy and meaning in your life, make it a priority to give others a sense of joy and meaning in their lives. If you want others to trust you, you have to be trustworthy and trust others. If you give people a chance, almost everyone will do the right thing. If you can't sell it, you'll never get the chance to do it. We do what we are incentivized to do—incentives in this instance are not necessarily monetary or external.

The best remedy for failure is to try again.

America's founding fathers envisioned our country built on self-government, with checks and balances via an elected executive, legislature, and independent judiciary, plus a free press. The fifth pillar supporting our country was, and is, reliance on the private sector to meet our economic needs. Entrepreneurs are the core of this fifth pillar. My hope is that, if this is your chosen path, your success will add to the economic well-being of yourself and this country.

FURTHER READING

1. *The One Minute Manager* by Kenneth Blanchard and Spencer Johnson, William Morrow, an imprint of HarperCollins Publishers, 1982.

2. *So You Want to be an Entrepreneur* by Jim Schell, Lights on Publishing, 2017.

3. *Winning the Talent Shift* by Berta Aldrich, Wiley, 2021.

4. *Rise of the Millennial Entrepreneur* by Joey Wilkes.

5. *The E-Myth Revisited* by Michael E. Gerber, HarperCollins, 1995.

6. *The Lean Startup* by Eric Ries, Currency, 2011.

7. *Corporate Value Creation* by Lawrence C. Karlson, Wiley, 2015.

APPENDIX 1

Successful companies thoughtfully memorialize their operating philosophy so it's clear to all their stakeholders. This is my former company, ERM's, corporate philosophy that guided all of our actions.

ERM'S PHILOSOPHY AND MISSION

- Our reason for being is to meet our clients' needs and to preserve and/or enhance our common environment; everything we do should relate to that mission.
- We want to provide creative and innovative solutions to environmental problems and opportunities that consider efficiency, reliability, and economy.
- We want to distinguish ourselves in the marketplace by providing services to management in all our business sectors.

- We foster a partnership mindset and organizational model and believe that we produce the best results through teamwork.

- We want to optimize results for our clients and the company on a global basis, as opposed to individual segments of our practice.

- We prize our entrepreneurial spirit and will continue to encourage our staff to develop their own market niches.

- We want to maintain as flat (and invisible) an organization as possible, encouraging senior staff to participate in project work.

- We strive to help each individual staff member realize their individual development goals.

- Integrity is an essential attribute for all staff and critical to our success as individual professionals and in our corporate business practices.

- We embrace excellence, creativity, efficiency, and service as the key goals in satisfying our clients' needs, as well as our own.

- We want to be part of the solution in making this a better world.

- We want everyone at our company to enjoy their work.

The following was ERM's Mission Statement laying out who we are, what we do, and who we serve.

- We will be a significant international provider of high-quality, comprehensive environmental management, science, and engineering services, maintaining a "balance" between private and public sectors.

- Within the private sector, initiatives will focus on major industrial clients while being selectively responsive to smaller organizations.

- Within the public sector, selected opportunities will be pursued to the extent they do not conflict with private sector work.

- We will be recognized for providing the highest level of service, responsiveness, and sensitivity to our clients' needs through application of science, engineering, and managerial creativity.

- Services will be provided from strategically located offices in key cities worldwide.

- We will provide a challenging professional environment that attracts and develops high-quality personnel and offers opportunities for fulfillment of personal and career goals.

- We will diversify into compatible business areas both geographically and functionally, providing services and products with strong potential for high near-term market share and with the growth and profit potential that will yield increased stability and market value over the longer term.

- We will meet our capital needs by generating better-than-average profits and through conservative use of debt.

APPENDIX 2

SHAREHOLDER AGREEMENT

Businesses with more than one owner should have a corporate lawyer-prepared shareholder agreement. The agreement should reflect the particulars of the business situation and the concerns and desires of the shareholders. The following is a list of the major sections in the ERM Agreement. It is included only to suggest some of the topics a typical shareholder agreement should consider.

TYPICAL CONTENT

1. Who Are the Parties to the Agreement?
2. Background of Agreement
3. Share Ownership

4. Application of Agreement
5. Legend on Share Certificates
6. Issuance and Sale of Additional Shares by the Company
7. Purchases by the Company
8. Disability
9. Death
10. Retirement
11. Departure Before Retirement
12. Right of First Refusal
13. Payment Terms
14. Deferred Payment
15. Fair Market Value
16. Election of Company to Purchase Shares of the Capital Stock
17. Covenant Not to Compete
18. Involuntary Transfer
19. Name Change
20. Severability
21. Waiver
22. Further Assurance
23. Governing Law
24. Genders: Headings: Plural: Person
25. Binding on Successors
26. Notices
27. Entire Agreement: Amendment
28. Execution in Counterparts

APPENDIX 3

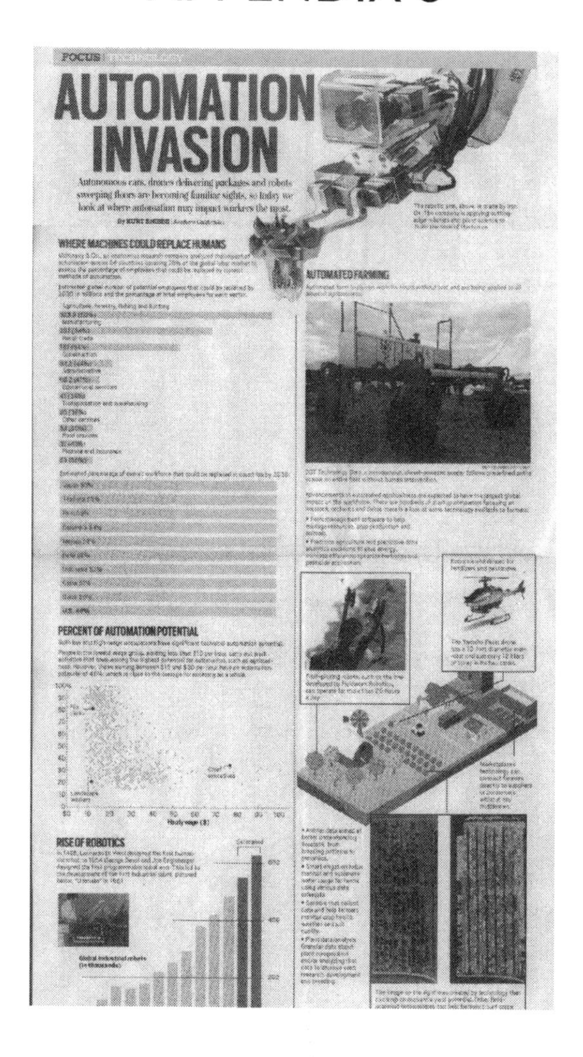

FOCUS

AUTOMATION INVASION

Autonomous cars, drones delivering packages and robots sweeping floors are becoming familiar sights, so today we look at where automation may impact workers the most.

WHERE MACHINES COULD REPLACE HUMANS

AUTOMATED FARMING

PERCENT OF AUTOMATION POTENTIAL

RISE OF ROBOTICS

Automation and its near-term impact on employment. Used with permission of Daily Local News, *February 22, 2020, page A8.*

Made in United States
Orlando, FL
27 January 2023